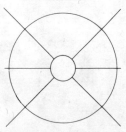

*Focus on Hinduism
and Buddhism*

*Robert A. McDermott
Series Editor*

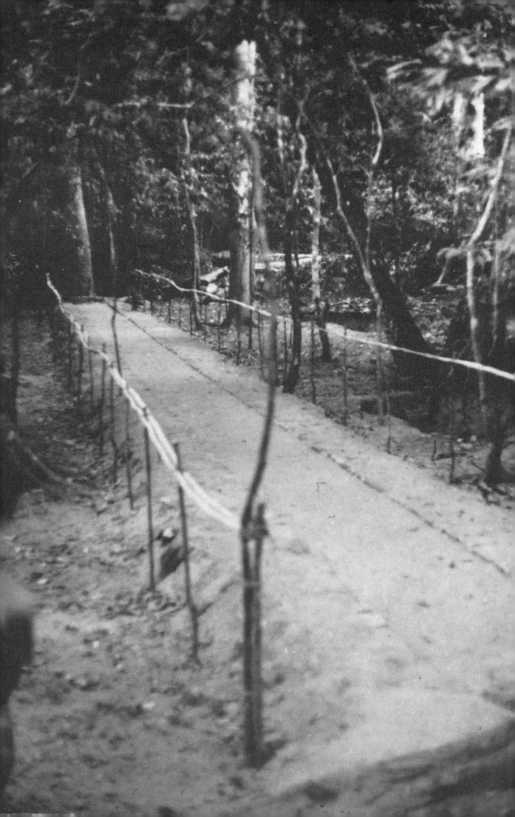

Spiritual Discipline in Hinduism, Buddhism, and the West

Harry M. Buck

ANIMA BOOKS, 1981

Buck, Harry Merwyn.
  Spiritual discipline in Hinduism, Buddhism, and the West.

  Bibliography: p.
  1. Spiritual life (Hinduism) 2. Spiritual life (Buddhism) 3. Spiritual life (Hinduism)—Study and teaching—Audio-visual aids. 4. Spiritual life (Buddhism)—Study and teaching—Audio-visual aids. I. Title.
BL1228.B83   294.3'444   81-12812
ISBN 0-89012-022-6   AACR2

This volume is part of a series of guides for the audio-visual materials useful for the study of Hinduism and Buddhism. Preparation and publication were made possible by a grant from the National Endowment for the Humanities to the Council on International and Public Affairs, Inc. (Ward Morehouse, President), with Robert A. McDermott as Project Director. Through the Endowment's provision for matching funds, this project was supported by the Ada Howe Kent Foundation and Baruch College, CUNY.

Printed in USA.

ANIMA BOOKS is a subdivision of Conococheague Associates, Inc., 1053 Wilson Avenue, Chambersburg, Pennsylvania 17201.

Foreword

THE AUTHOR of this guide shares with the other scholars who have contributed to this series* a deep commitment to the value of Asian religions as a way of life as well as a set of teachings. Further, Professor Buck was learning from Hindu and Buddhist spiritual masters long before it was fashionable to do so. He was a student of Swami Akhilananda, of the Ramakrishna Vedanta Society in Boston, in the 1950s while he was an Instructor of Biblical History, Literature and Interpretation at Wellesley College. Throughout the '60s and '70s, in ashrams, monasteries and universities, he studied the major spiritual disciplines of Hinduism and Buddhism, both in their native environment and in their American incarnations. This range of experience is manifest in the catholicity and sobriety both of his essay and of his recommendations for the use of audio-visual materials.

The above remarks on the author of this guide are rather personal because of the intensely personal and inevitably subjective nature of spiritual discipline. Note that this is not a claim that Harry Buck should be looked to as a spiritual master, or even as a dedicated practitioner, but simply that he has the requisite experience and learning for the purposes of this guide. Bluntly stated, Harry Buck has been at this work long enough, and with sufficient range of experience, that he is less likely than the rest of us to confuse the finger pointing to the moon for the moon itself. More specifically, since he combines a scholar's knowledge of classical texts and teachings, with a personal affinity for spiritual discipline, and a professor's pedagogical sense of materials appropriate for undergraduate study, we can take seriously both his essay and his recommendations concerning the use of audio-visual resources.

Perhaps the surest sign of the author's mature perspective in these complex matters is his sober caution: "Meditation and spiritual practices are elusive. If talking about them doesn't suffice, neither does a proliferation of pictures and sounds" (page 55). All three of these instruments — words, pictures and sounds — are shown to be both useful and ultimately

---

*See Diana Eck, *Darśana: The Visual in the Hindu Religious Tradition*; Richard B. Pilgrim, *Buddhism and the Arts of Japan*; Donald K. Swearer, *Buddhism and Society in Southeast Asia*. These four guides, in turn, presuppose *Focus on Hinduism* and *Focus on Buddhism*, two comprehensive critical surveys, respectively, of the Hindu and Buddhist religious traditions. All of these works are under the general editorship of Robert A. McDermott, and are published by Anima Publications, 1981.

inadequate. To treat them as solutions would be to mistake the finger for the moon, but to give up on them entirely would be like regarding the finger and the moon as illusory. Professor Buck's essay not ony affirms the instrumental value of words, pictures and sounds, but attempts to develop a positive relationship between them.

As with spiritual discipline itself, Professor Buck's essay strives to keep in focus the complex relationship between the means and the aims of spiritual discipline. We should note that neither lends itself to visual presentation or verbal description. At best, and then with caution and humility, we can attempt to match the means — words, pictures and sounds — to the aims — "authentic immediacy, concentration on the present moment, and relaxed intensity" (page 50). Throughout his essay Professor Buck draws on the well established words and sounds, shapes and symbols, of classic teachings, and then relates them to contemporary teachers, groups and audio-visual presentations. This juxtaposition typifies the methodology and intent of the entire guide: by surprising combinations — whether of classical and contemporary, East and West, temporal and eternal, absolute and relative, words and pictures, sounds and silence — this essay encourages the reader/viewer to move beyond the habits of passive thinking, listening and viewing to within closer reach of the immediacy necessary for spiritual realization.

As valuable as these juxtapositions may be, however, both the essay and the "Guide to Audio-Visual Resources" provide numerous recommendations which aim not so much at spiritual insight as at intellectual knowledge. In short, despite his sympathy with the efficacy of spiritual disciplines, this guide mirrors its author's fundamental commitment to the academic study of religious experience, one essential and frequently confusing ingredient of which is spiritual discipline. It is the contribution of this guide that it enables the reader/user to gain both an academic and a personal understanding of spiritual disciplines, and to do so in a way which utilizes sight and sound as well as word.

While Professor Buck's essay can stand on its own as an introduction to the varieties of spiritual disciplines, its full value awaits its implementation in relation to the films recommended in the "Guide to Audio-Visual Resources." The essay, in turn, will be enhanced by the serious viewing and analysis of these films. Ultimately, of course, the respective functions of both the guide and the films will be realized to the extent that the user of these materials begins to penetrate the mysterious methods and effects included in spiritual discipline.

Robert A. McDermott
Series Editor

Contents

Preface

OF WHAT should the study of religion consist?

Colleges and universities traditionally emphasize the study of written materials, and most religious traditions have a body of sacred literature that can be analyzed, exegeted, and studied with critical sophistication. Social scientists add what they call field research to their studies, and religious traditions have cultic ceremonies that can be seen, music that can be heard, and objects that can be photographed. In addition, religions tend to develop elaborate philosophies and theologies, frequently complex intellectual explanations, and sets of beliefs. These are fair game for the academic student of religion, reinforcing a bias compatible with the idea of the university and with Christian scholasticism.

Scientists in the university insist on yet another component in their teaching, experience in the laboratory, where students can confront phenomena directly — without words, without labels, without explanation. A laboratory approach rarely appears in the teaching of religion. Yet within virtually every great religious tradition, there is an experiential dynamic. If a scholar observes only texts, ceremonies, artifacts, and theologies, the inner spirituality that has kept most important traditions alive will be invisible. This dimension of religion, called here *spiritual discipline*, is not easily accessible by books, nor can it be conveniently photographed. Spiritual practices must be experienced, a frightening prospect to many professors who have striven for so many generations to make their field "respectable" and "objective."

To study about meditation is one thing, and there are many good books.* To experience meditation is something entirely different, but it is difficult to accomplish. One can enroll in the Aurobindo Ashram in Pondicherry in South India or sit for several months at the Zen monastery at Kita Kamakura in Japan, but these are unreasonable demands, not at all comparable to a chemistry laboratory that meets four hours a week on campus. If the instructor is trained, spiritual practices can be taught in class, but student experience will be limited to the one or two types of spiritual discipline familiar to the instructor. What, then, are we to do if we are not to neglect this important part of our studies?

At the present time judiciously selected and carefully used motion picture film is the best medium we have. Even a production lacking in artistic sophistication can provide a sense of presence and participation. Films are

*Bibliographical references are numbered consecutively, beginning on page 53. A bibliography of useful books begins on page 66.

not a substitute for scholarship or rigorous teaching, but used with care they can be important components of both.

This book provides a framework for the incorporation of motion pictures in creative teaching. Most of the book is an essay on spiritual practices, especially meditation, with footnote reference to films that will be useful in classroom instruction or for private viewing. Numbered endnotes point to supplementary reading material. The second part of the book describes selected films themselves, prefaced by some observations on their proper use. A glossary of important terms and a bibliography follow.

Fully as important as a knowledge of the contents of various films to be used will be the preparation of the viewers. Opposition to the serious consideration of religious experience that characterizes many schools of theology is reinforced by the prejudice against audio-visual "aids," as they are contemptuously called in many intellectual circles.

In reaction to the rationalism of a previous generation, our own age can be charged with trusting personal experience to excess. When the ontological framework of an age no longer supports the life-needs of its people, one can expect a frantic grasping at whatever esoteric cult seems to offer salvation. When the Pax Romana fell apart, for example, foreign cults of every description became popular. Our own age presents a similar picture. Traditional Western systems of belief and practice fail to sustain the needs of many contemporary persons, and the rapid growth of fundamentalist cults — Christian, Muslim, Hindu, and Buddhist — only underscores this observation. They are part of the same phenomena witnessed in the guru-centered movements with their charismatic leaders who can compel absolute obedience to their authoritative directives. These phenomena too are part of the picture and have a duty to present spiritual disciplines in a thoughtful and sensitive perspective.

This volume focuses on spiritual practices in Hindu and Buddhist contexts, with only passing reference to phenomena elsewhere. Christian saints like Caterina de Siena or Teresa, Augustine or Thomas à Kempis, are not our immediate concern. The shadow of Al Ghazalli or Rabi'ā in the Islamic Sufi tradition will scarcely cross our path. The Jewish Kabbalah, to say nothing of modern figures like Martin Buber or Abraham Heschel, will be virtually ignored. All of these, and many other Jewish, Christian, and Muslim mystics, are fascinating examples of how "the spirit bloweth where it listeth," cutting across all divisions. We are, however, concerned more with names like Patanjali, Bodhidharma, the anonymous authors of the *Visuddhimagga* or the *Satipaṭṭhāna Sūtta* or even of the *Chandogya Upaniṣad*, or in more modern times Swami Akhilananda, Daisetz T. Suzuki, the Venerable D. Piyananda, and others.*[1]

---

* *The Path of Meditation* can be useful to introduce the whole field. It is tied to no particular tradition, except that of the narrator's own bias. *The Art of Meditation* and *Awakening* will also be useful. These films are described in more detail in Appendix I of this book, and these descriptions should be consulted before films are used.

Whatever else it is — and clearly there is much more — religion is a human experience, intensely involving whole persons in a response to what has been experienced as Ultimate Concern or Ultimate Reality. In this light systems of beliefs and collections of scriptures take on meaning. To ignore this emphasis is to invite a question about why such beliefs or practices would ever become popular at all. Although this volume is written by an author who believes in the importance and value of many of the practices described, it is not a plea for coversion. If you wish to remain simply as an observer, these films will be useful. How far students or teachers choose to embrace such practices must remain matters of individual decision. This treatment will, however, stress the importance of authenticity in any response. The sea is vast. Plunge in if you like. Sit on the shore if you prefer, but look carefully. Either way is valid.

What, then, about the West? In American cities devotees of Lord Kṛṣṇa can usually be found in many public places. Sokagakkai, a Japanese movement springing from the Buddhist saint Nichiren, has established many centers. Wherever there are concentrations of oriental people there will be Mahāyāṇa congregations. Major cities have Vedānta centers, Buddhist Vihāras, and other places where meditation can be taught and seriously pursued with little fanfare or public notice. Zen centers are increasingly available.[2] Few films deal with Western practices, and, therefore, most of this treatment will describe Hindu and Buddhist practices in India, South and Southeast Asia, and Japan. Our approach is that of westerners seeking understanding of eastern practices.

This preface should conclude with thanks to certain persons whose contributions have been significant. Insightful comments on many of the films were made by Laura Barrett and Carol Kipe, recent graduates of Wilson College. My evaluations were significantly affected by their reactions. Students in a January Term course at Gettysburg College, which I shared with Professor Harold Dunkelberger, assisted in some film evaluations. A sophomore paper by Mary Elizabeth Campell, another recent Wilson College graduate, provided a valuable perspective in developing this book.

Perhaps the decisive influence in my attitude toward the use of films was derived from many contacts with Professor Melvin Levison of Brooklyn College and Cynthia Allen of New York. When Professor John Borelli of College of Mount Saint Vincent, Professor Ewert Cousins of Fordham University, Dr. Daniel Goleman of *Psychology Today*, Dr. Jean Houston of the Foundation for Mind Research, or Dr. Frank Podgorski of the *Journal of Dharma* read these words they will undoubtedly recognize some of their language that I have unconsciously assimilated. I shared a panel with them at the American Academy of Religion in 1977 and have discussed these matters with them on other occasions. Dr. Rita Gross, University of Wisconsin-Eau Claire, suggested important books.

I would be unforgivably remiss if I did not acknowledge a debt beyond measure to certain mahātmas of our own age, whom it has been my privilege to know. The Venerable D. Piyananda, recently of the Washington Buddhist Vihāra and now in retirement in Sri Lanka, and Professor Hajime Nakamura of the University of Tokyo remain constant sources of inspiration. I deeply miss the presence of Swami Akhilananda of the Ramakrishna Vedanta Society in Boston, my first teacher in such matters, and Daisetz T. Suzuki, citizen of the world.

CHAPTER 1

The Practice of Religion

WESTERN STUDENTS of religion, as well as a good many easterners, need a radical reorientation to understand meditation and spiritual practices. Particularly the terms *self* and *God*, as subject and object or as object and subject, will be misleading. Spiritual practices of eastern religions do not proceed from the same starting point as Western philosophy.

Three Paths

Hindu pandits traditionally identify three *margas* or *yogas* as paths to realization: *karma-yoga*, the path of ethical living and cultic ceremonies; *jñana-yoga*, the way of understanding and study, frequently involving active contemplation; and *bhakti-yoga*, the route of loving devotion and service. Despite personal preferences, it is usually maintained that no one of these ways is "better" than the others, and most practicing Hindus combine aspects of all three. This use of the word *yoga* is to distinguish three paths to the realization of the goal. The term is used differently when it refers to such practices as *hatha* yoga or *raja* yoga, specific Hindu methods prescribed in religious texts, chiefly those of Patanjali.

What we are calling spiritual practices is at least karma, because the practice of religion is something done, and something done with the body. Hatha yoga training, for example, teaches specific bodily postures called *āsanas*. Zazen, in Zen Buddhist practice, requires strict control of the body. An ashram, like a Christian monastery, prescribes rigorous schedules involving physical labor and limitations on sleep and bodily comfort. Usually there are restrictions on diet, sex, drugs or alcohol.*

Jñana, which basically means to have knowledge, consists of far more than what is connoted by the English word *study*. It is, to be sure, a kind of intellectualization, but more is involved; the "more" is quiet contemplation. Students confronting the Chandogya Upaniṣad, for example, tend to be totally confused by the first several chapters. They do not "make sense" until they are seen not as treatises for study but as guides for contemplation. This upaniṣad cannot be learned; it must be realized, and realization involves *jñana*.

---

*Some illustrations of these practices will be found in several films, but usually embedded in portrayals of other phenomena. *Hinduism and the Song of God* contains some interesting footage. *Buddhism: The Land of the Disappearing Buddha* has several scenes showing zen practices and two short sequences on zazen sitting. *Zen in Ryoku-in* may also be helpful. With careful preparation, one could use parts of the *Art of Meditation* and *The Path*.

Probably the most visible side of spiritual practices can be seen in the *bhakti* movements, loving devotion to a particular deity. Chanting the names of God, being caught up in ecstatic states of consciousness, even the mortification of the body in fulfillment of a vow are all highly visible parts of devotion. A caution is in order in trying to use film footage to portray bhakti. Only the externalia of a cult can be photographed, and it is easy to become so enamored of the performance as to miss the essence.

What, then, do we mean by terms like *meditation* and *spiritual practices*? They are ways of living that seek restoration of wholeness. *Wholeness, holiness,* and *health* are interrelated, not simply by etymology but in life, lived fully. Because we are discussing practices, we are perforce dealing with actions (*praxis*), whereby the body will be the vehicle for the development of the whole self. Historically, religions have begun here, for it has been observed that before religions were thought out they were danced out.

Practices, however, are not simply techniques. A teacher of meditation does not give the kind of instruction one would give to a worker on an assembly line — how to do this or how to do that. There will be instruction in proper procedure and correction of errors, but a better analogy is instruction on how to play a musical instrument. Some skills can be demonstrated, some mechanisms can be learned, but all instruction is useless, unless the student brings a developed artistic awareness to practice.

The term *meditation* poses difficulty. From the root *med* many words were derived ranging from *medesthai* (Greek, "to think about") to *mēdesthai* (Greek, "to care about") to *mederi* (Latin, "to cure"). By 1700 the English word came to mean to fix attention by studying and pondering a particular situation. All these definitions carry far too many connotations of thinking, a mental activity as opposed to a physical one. In the spiritual practices of Asia, meditation captures a whole person.

The word *spiritual* may be even more elusive. The *Oxford English Dictionary* says simply, "pertaining to sacred concerns,"[3] an unsatisfactory attempt. *Spirit* translates a variety of words: *pneuma* (Greek), *ruach* (Hebrew), *nefesh* (Hebrew), and *anima* (Sanskrit and Latin), to name a few, all of them designating some form of air or life-giving breath. *Spirit*, therefore, emerged with the meaning "the animating or vital principle" in human life,[4] not unlike the Hindu term *prāna*. Spiritual practices, then, many of them beginning with an emphasis on breathing, are properly to be understood as ways of uniting my little self with the great life-giving Self in wholeness. Such a statement is mere words, confusing words, until one has practiced long enough to retain the faculty of attention and reorient conceptions about the nature of selfhood and ego.

Knowledge can be imparted, but the knowledge needed (*jñāna*) must be direct and immediate, that is, not mediated, but the result of experience. It cannot be the simple memorization of texts or the recitation of facts, as illustrated in this famous conversation between Sanatkumāra and Nārada.

> Nārada approached Sanatkumāra (as a pupil) and said: "Venerable Sir, please teach me."
> Sanatkumāra said to him: "Please tell me what you already know. Then I shall tell you what is beyond."
> Nārada said: "Venerable Sir, I know the Rig-Veda, the Yajur-Veda, the Sāma-Veda, the Atharva-Veda as the fourth (Veda), the epics (Purāṇas) and ancient lore (Itihāsa) as the fifth, the Veda of the Vedas (i.e., grammar), the rules of the sacrifices by which the Manes are gratified, the science of numbers, the science of portents, the science of time, logic, ethics, etymology, Brahma-vidyā (i.e., the science of pronunciation, ceremonials, prosody, etc.), the science of elemental spirits, the science of weapons, astronomy, the science of serpents, and the fine arts. All this I know, Venerable Sir.
> "But Venerable Sir, with all this, I know words only; I do not know the Self. I have heard from men like you that he who knows the Self overcomes sorrow. I am one afflicted with sorrow. Do you, Venerable Sir, help me to cross over to the other side of sorrow."
> Sanatkumāra said to him: "Whatever you have read is only a name."[5]

The needed skills combine karma, jñāna, and bhakti. On occasion these practices bridge the gap between Christians and Buddhists and between Hindus and Muslims, not because they unite religions — they don't — but because they bring together human beings who may be from different backgrounds and conditioning. It is not surprising, then, that contemplatives from one traditional background find deeper fellowship with similarly minded people from quite opposing religious perspectives than they do with other representatives of their own denominations whose practices are more conventional.

Each of the several spiritual disciplines has its own distinctiveness, and there is a sense in which each one can be understood — and practiced — only in its own context. C. G. Jung argued strongly against attempting a syncretism between Western ontologies and Eastern practices, despite his profound respect for Eastern methods of meditation. On the other hand, the differences between the great religions often hinge on theology, metaphysics, and an explanation of "how things are." The ontologies of Christianity and Buddhism, Islam and Hinduism, may be totally incompatible; the effects of spiritual practices of Christians, Buddhists, Muslims, and Hindus may produce a real community with very similar results.

Virtually every religion, then, has developed some dimensions in depth, and because that depth has become an important goal — in some cases the only goal — spiritual disciplines have evolved. We cannot overstress the idea of discipline, which means teaching and instruction and control. It is not left to chance. It can be taught. It can be communicated. It can be passed from teacher to student, from guru to siṣya.

The Sword of the Spirit and the Arm of the Flesh

"The sword of the spirit," said George Butterick many years ago, "is moved by the arm of the flesh." Although some gospels maintain that true worshipers "will worship the Father in spirit and in truth," implying that nonbodily aspects of worship are "purer" than those involving the pollution of the flesh, it is truer to reality to assert that religious experience involves total beings in their totality. The antiseptic and verbal nature of much Protestant worship and not the more ecstatic bodily postures of the so-called cults may in fact be the aberration.

Joachim Wach used to insist that a religious experience involved what he called a total response of a total person to what was seen as Ultimate Reality. He stressed each word. The reponse is not a reaction, not something that happens automatically. It is total — not merely mind, or emotions, or body — but all of them. It is the total response of total persons with such intensity that long-range results follow.

Wach preferred the term *Ultimate Reality* to the word *God*. God as transcendent person is a frame of reference conspicuously absent from these films, and even though the term *God* will be used over and over in this essay, in the context of Eastern spirituality it rarely implies the totally separate personal being that the word designates in Judaism, Christianity, or Islam. The monotheistic traditions have indeed developed great spiritual mystics, like the Christian Bonaventura or more recently Thomas Merton, but the basic cleavage between God and the worshiper that is so vital to monotheism may prove an initial stumbling block for a westerner trying to enter into the nonduality of much of Eastern spirituality.*[6]

The separation of human life into such divisions as body, mind, emotions, spirit, or whatever other faculties one wishes to designate, can effectively isolate one from reality. There is little agreement among various schools of meditation on what constitutes a human person, on what is the self. Most classical systems, however, do recommend particular environments for the meditative process, an ashram, a monastery, a retreat, at least some quiet place away from the noise of everyday commerce. They may differ widely on the importance of certain postures and practices or on the relation between morality and spiritual progress, or on many other issues. Nontheless, some kind of training that involves both mind and body is usual.

Although the metaphysical basis may vary considerably from system to system, within the context of Hindu and Buddhist practices — the scope

Be Ye Lamps Unto Yourselves is a useful film in this context.

of this guide — some attention must be paid to the intricate relationship between self, mind, and body. Western students have been conditioned by generations of belief to assume, usually without question, that somewhere in my body there is an "I," a "myself." This ego-entity, often called a soul, directs traffic in the complex organism, the body, which expresses its wishes. We assume a certain permanence and consistency in this ego, a self-unity, in which I am set apart from you, and I can define myself because I am not-you. If, then, as we have been taught, "man is made in the image of God," God must also have the qualities of a distinct, individual person.

Moreover, God must be distinct and separate, unlike anything else. Theological systems from *neti-neti* in India to the Jewish Moses Maimonides define God only in terms of what "He" is not. This is monotheism, not because there is only one God — Advaita Vedanta would not disagree with such a statement — but because God is absolutely distinct, separate, unique.

This book is not the place to discuss Hindu and Buddhist psychology in any detail.[7] We are more concerned with the communication of such a frame of reference. How shall it be taught? Not in words only. It is not taught; it is demonstrated. When one pays careful attention to breathing — in and out, in and out — one becomes aware at a level far more significant than that of wakeful consciousness that one does not own any breath. It is mine for an instant, and then I expel it, and there is little distinction between my breath and yours and the air around. A few hours spent in careful attention to breath and breathing will teach the metaphysics more effectively than a semester of lectures. When the body experiences, the spirit understands.

The Body

When the Buddha outlined his famous Eightfold Path, he began with Right Seeing. Without some sort of vision of a goal there will be very little spiritual progress and no movement. But once this first step has been taken, the following five steps involve specific actions:

— Right aspiration, a resolve to do those things that lead to the goal and abstain from those that do not, in Hindu terms to embrace *dharma* and shun *adharma*,

— Right speech,

— Right conduct,

— Right means of livelihood,

— Right effort.

Only then does the Noble Eightfold Path talk about what many persons regard as meditation and spiritual practices.

— Right mindfulness,

— Right meditation.

Spiritual practices, therefore, do not begin with meditative techniques. There is no instant road to nirvāṇa. It begins with a reorientation of one's life, the uses to which one puts one's body. The classic manual of Theravāda meditation, the *Vissuddhimagga*,[8] opens with a long discussion of *sīla* ("morality") before it mentions any meditative techniques. Purity, concentration, and insight are three kinds of development that must take place simultaneously. So one begins with bodily actions.

There are always preparation rituals, usually involving personal cleanliness and order in the surroundings. Water is a pervasive image,* but one author uses the analogy of a kerosene lamp. If the glass chimney and the wick and the fuel are dirty, the light will be uncertain, but when the wick has been trimmed and the glass cleaned, clear vision is easy.[9] Before beginning any formal program in meditation, one is usually instructed in quite menial tasks. In the Theravāda tradition, this means observing the five precepts: not killing, not stealing, not engaging in improper sexual conduct, not lying, and not drinking intoxicants. For monks there are 227 prohibitions that regulate virtually all aspects of life for a bhikkhu.

In the Buddhist Eightfold Path one begins at a simple, physical level. "Acts of purity are meant to produce a calmed and subdued mind. The purity of morality has only the purity of mind as its goal."[10] And so, after Right Seeing and Right Aspirations, both preliminary to all else, the next step on the Path, Right Speech, is required. When one learns to regulate speech so as not to harm another, one has won a great victory over oneself. By controlling speech I have already dealt a blow to my concept of ego, that center around which my whole cosmos revolved before setting out on the Path. "I" am no longer the center of "my" world.

Right Conduct — the fourth step — follows immediately, proceeding to Right Livelihood; some lifestyles simply are not appropriate to the spiritual life. Because the body does respond to careful training, strengths gained by spiritual disciplines are not always beneficial. Techniques that work can be taught, and one of the most serious flaws of many popular — one might even say commercialized — meditative movements is the notion that a charismatic guru can teach a technique that makes minimal demands and produces hedonistic satisfaction. Right Effort, then, follows Right Livelihood as the sixth step, and only then does one proceed to Right Mindfulness and Right Meditation.†

The term *spiritual discipline* is well-chosen. A disappointment to those eager for instant states of hallucination and immediate solutions to problems, the practice of the meditative life is about as exciting as the practice of the violin — hour after hour of training the body to respond correctly,

---

*Water is an image in many of these films: *The Art of Meditation*, and *The Flow of Zen* in particular use many pictures of water.

†In connection with showing *Buddhism: The Land of the Disappearing Buddha*, one could ask viewers whether Zen techniques might be used for unworthy ends. *A Contemporary Guru — Rajnish* has valuable insights on distinguishing meditative movements with depth from those that may be exploitative.

freely, and easily. A beginning driver must concentrate carefully on which pedal to push, which lever to pull to control the car. I do not want to ride with anyone in heavy traffic, however, until all those motions have become so much a part of the body's response that attention can be totally on the traffic pattern. This is what is meant by the freedom to do what one pleases. Without the necessary discipline, I am incapable of doing anything I please.

In the following chapter we shall develop brief descriptions of various spiritual paths, but the one thing they share in common is keen attention to very mundane activities. There is nothing unusual about reaching for a pencil on my desk and beginning to write with it. But it is unusual for me to *experience* myself reaching for that pencil — to *feel* consciously the actions of my fingers and what happens to my muscles as I make them obey the desire to record my thoughts. So with drinking a glass of water or walking down the street.*

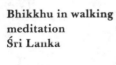

Bhikkhu in walking
meditation
Śri Lanka

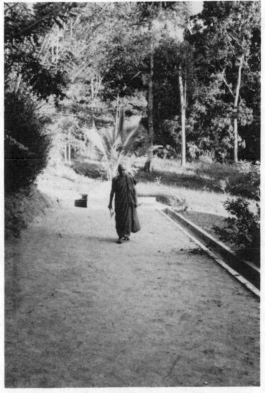

*Walking is a form of meditation, and several films show feet walking, perhaps because it is an easy subject to photograph. Much is to be learned, however, from attention to walking, and students can be asked to observe the feet in several films, particularly in *Buddhism: Be Ye Lamps Unto Yourselves, Buddhism: Footprints of the Buddha, Buddhism: The Path to Enlightenment,* and *The Smile.*

The Effects of Meditation

Meditation is associated with other religious practices, but in essence it is a bodily act, a careful retraining of the faculty of attention to let go of all distractions from the present moment. A Buddhist system known as Vipassana Meditation stresses first "Bare Attention," simply paying close attention to everything about the present moment, as Sri Baba Ram Dass says it, to "Be Here, Now." How our attention jumps like a monkey from thought to thought, concern to concern, mostly imaginary, while we miss our present opportunities! If we think that meditation ought to produce psychic effects similar to a combination of Götterdammerung and the 1812 Overture, we need to be reminded that instead of extraordinary actions, what is involved is extraordinary attention to very ordinary actions.

It is necessary for us to keep the constant way. Zen is not some kind of excitement, but concentration on our usual everyday routine. If you become too busy and too excited, your mind becomes rough and ragged. This is not good. If possible, try to be always calm and joyful and keep yourself from excitement. Usually we become busier and busier, day by day, year by year, especially in our modern world. If we revisit old, familiar places after a long time, we are astonished by the changes. It cannot be helped. But if we become interested in some excitement, or in our own change, we will become completely involved in our busy life, and we will be lost. But if your mind is calm and constant, you can keep yourself away from the noisy world even though you are in the midst of it. In the midst of noise and change, your mind will become quiet and stable.[11]

Spiritual discipline is a slow process, and it does not yield rapid results. When used for bizarre purposes and selfish ends, it defeats its own values, not because it does not work, but precisely because it does, and in working, apart from the necessary discipline and resolution, without Right Seeing, it can reinforce my sense of ego-satisfaction and lead to further frustration. But used in context, some observable results can be demonstrated.

Daniel Goleman found in psychological research that meditators rise more rapidly to stress situations than do nonmeditators, and they subside more quickly.

The anxious person meets life's normal events as though they were crises. Each minor happening increases his tension, and his tension in turn magnifies the next ordinary event — a deadline, a doctor's appointment, an interview — into a threat. Because the anxious person's body stays mobilized after one event has passed, he has a lower threat threshold for the next. Had he been in a relaxed state, he would have taken the next event in stride.

The meditator handles stress in a way that breaks up the threat-arousal-threat spiral. The meditator relaxes after a challenge passes more often than the non-meditator. This makes him unlikely to see innocent occurrences as harmful. He perceives threat more accurately, and reacts with arousal only when necessary. Once aroused, his rapid recovery makes him less likely than the anxious person to see the next deadline as threat.[12]

Some changes can actually be quantified. Even a simple biofeedback machine can confirm the ability of a meditator to produce alpha waves, brain waves of a frequency different from those of "ordinary" consciousness, and it can detect galvanic skin responses demonstrating the effects of different kinds of breathing or relaxation of tension. The sympathetic nervous system increases its activity when there is fear, anger or tension.

An alteration of consciousness is certainly a result of spiritual practices, but altered states of consciousness (ASC) are not its goal. To be sure, whatever the meditative tradition, a retrained consciousness is involved, and the world is perceived differently as a result of the regime. But to emphasize enjoyment of a trance state is not really a changed viewpoint at all. It is simply the same old values turned upside down, as an examination of the plethora of popular sectarian movements ministering to such urges will soon reveal.

The next chapter, "Paths to the Goal," will examine a few selected types of spiritual discipline, each in its own context, before returning to more general observations.

CHAPTER 2

Paths to the Goal

DESPITE MANY similarities among the spiritual disciplines of the world, each tradition has developed its special methods. Although we have argued that there is a substratum of spirituality independent of any religious metaphysic, it is also true that in any well-developed spirituality there is an inner consistency.

Beginning with the insight of Elijah, who found that God (Yahweh) was not to be found in the earthquake, the wind, and the fire (I Kings 19) where all nature gods were to be found, but in the personal, political, and social affairs of men and women, there have developed three great monotheistic traditions: Judaism, Christianity, and Islam. The essence of monotheism is not simply that there is only one God as opposed to several but that God is absolutely distinct and separate from the world, created by God. In this context meditation is not natural. Prayer and obedience are more appropriate. But all three of these great monotheisms developed spiritual practices, incorporating them into one great spiritual stream.

In Judaism there is the Kabbalah, a "hidden" tradition, supposedly transmitted through Abraham, David, the prophets, and perhaps the Essenes and other mystical groups whose experience with God was direct and immediate. In some medieval legends, Jesus is also a transmitter of the Kabbalah. Kabbalism sees many levels of reality, each embodying successive states of consciousness. Kabbalistic teaching aims to conduct the soul of the aspirant to higher levels of consciousness and uses figures from the Hebrew scriptures allegorically to this end. The true Exodus from Egypt, then, is the escape of the soul from lower levels of consciousness and its entry into higher stages.

In common with many eastern systems of meditation, the Kabbalist, instructed by his *maggid*, whose function is similar to that of a guru, learns to concentrate on one-pointed subjects. Kabbalist techniques are, in effect, extensions of the normal prayers of Judaism, but with a different end, called *devekut*, the cleaving of the soul to God himself, the transformation of the ordinary man into *zaddik* (a saint who has escaped his personal ego).

> The qualities of one who has attained his station include equanimity, indifference to praise or blame, a sense of being alone with God, and prophecy. The ego's will is submerged in the divine will

so that one's acts serve God rather than a limited self. He need no longer study Torah, for he has *become* Torah.[13]

Although it shares many similarities with Hindu and Buddhist disciplines — the merging of the ego with God and the Torah and the retraining of the soul to enter higher levels of consciousness — it never negates its Jewish monotheistic background, and the imagery of its meditative practices comes directly from Jewish scriptures.

Christianity, which grew up first in a Jewish context and later moved to a Hellenistic environment is an interesting syncretism between Jewish monotheism and Hellenistic mystery religions, many of them of Asian origin, with the addition of its distinctive theological feature, Christology. Christian monasteries, perhaps patterned deliberately by St. Benedict on Buddhist examples, went farther than Kabbalism in the direct experience of God — through Christ. Devotion to Christ, and devotion to the Blessed Mother quickly took on many of the features of Indian *bhakti*, with a constant remembrance of God. By the fourth century A.D. there were Christian hermits in the Egyptian desert, and Thomas Merton, who made the Trappist monastery in Kentucky well known, observes that "what is today practiced as 'prayer' in Christian churches is but one — albeit the surviving one — of a range of more intense contemplative practices."[14] Here a mantra is repeated, *Kyrie eleison* ("Lord have mercy on me") or the so-called Jesus Prayer, an expanded form of the same idea.

Like the followers of the Visuddhimagga, the Desert Fathers and the early monks stressed purity of life. Generally Christian monks do not meditate in the strictest sense of the word; they pray and work. Nevertheless, instructions given in the Benedictine orders and their derivatives are not at all out of harmony with instructions given in a Buddhist Vihāra, except, perhaps, for the Christological emphasis in the monastery.

Islam also developed a mystical tradition, known as Sufism, and such great figures as Al Hujwiri and Al Ghazalli taught spiritualities on a very high level. Sufis learned to dance and to whirl, by which means a trance state could be induced. Chiefly, however, they learned to polish the soul, to use Al Hujwiri's term, and after a series of purifications, to concentrate on spiritual stations, the last of which merged into a "god-given state." Sufis, however, were influenced by Hindus, as Christian monastics were influenced by Buddhists. Both have had difficulties in coming to terms with their more orthodox brethren, as the Kabbalists have also remained on the fringes of Judaism.

In dealing with meditation and spiritual practices, it is essential to be aware of their appearance in the monotheistic systems, but the focus of this study must be on the Dhamma of the Buddha and the Yoga of the Hindus.

The Yoga of Hinduism

The term *yoga* (akin to English *yoke*) can be used in a variety of ways, since its basic meaning is some method of yoking the individual with

Reality. Thus, we were able to mention three *yogas*: *karma, jñāna, and bhakti* to describe the three main routes to Indian spirituality. In this sense, virtually everything in Hinduism is yoga: temple ceremonies, home pūjas, bhajan singing, ritual bathing, and so on. In line with the criteria developed in Chapter 1 of this book, we have excluded these practices, even though they are often photographed.*

After most of the great upaniṣads had been developed, Hindu spiritual practices acquired considerable sophistication. Occasionally combined with other systems, *yoga* came to designate a particular kind of Indian philosophy and practice, codified in a manual, the *Yoga Sūtras*, composed by Patanjali, probably in the early centuries A.D. Patanjali's name is inextricably linked with *yoga* as used in Hinduism, and even American Transcendental Meditation makes use of it. Patanjali's Yoga came to be regarded as one of the six official philosophies (*darśanas*) in India.

The goal of yoga can be reached only by controlling mental activity completely. Whereas certain forms of Buddhism aim at observation, yoga aims at control. The goal is a state of pure consciousness, wherein all duality is transcended by a mind that has bridged the gap in *samādhi*, in which the yogin's awareness merges with the object of meditation.

Rigorous discipline and training still the thought waves of the mind to let one know oneself as one really is, having overcome the illusion of being separate from God. The arduous bodily and mental requirements prescribed by the Yoga Aphorisms are very demanding, and there is a similarity to the prescriptions of the *Visuddhimagga*, which we have already seen. Patanjali's *Aṣṭāṅga Yoga* also has eight steps, beginning with *yama* ("restraint") and *niyama* ("observance") which are not unlike the demand for *sīla*, moral and physical purity. This preparation is followed by *āsana*, meaning both sitting and meditation and postures, frequently involving elaborate physical training, some of it gymnastics. Along with *āsana* goes *prāṇāyāma*, the control of the breath. Here the breath is not merely observed; elaborate techniques have been developed to control it, some actually altering the oxygen supply to the brain, producing by that mechanical-chemical means altered states of consciousness.

Following *āsana* and *prāṇāyāma*, *pratyāhāra* ("sense withdrawal") is a means of actually disconnecting the senses. Now the yogi can concentrate without interruption on a fixed point. The final three steps, which Patanjali called *limbs*, lead to the goal: *dhāraṇā* ("concentration") and *dhyāna* ("meditation," the word from which the Japanese word *zen* is derived) lead to the first stages of *samādhi*. When the final level of *samādhi* is

---

Consecration of a Temple is the only such film we have included, although there are others. Prof. H. Daniel Smith of Syracuse University has produced a series of short studies of Hindu ritual, and the *Wedding of the Goddess* is also useful. Among the films we have included, *Aura of Divinity* shows some devotional practices that touch on the phenomena described here. *Hinduism* and *The Song of God* are organized around the three main yogas, and *Hinduism: Many Paths to One God* contains many useful segments.

reached, it is said to be "without seed." The self, finally liberated, exists in perfect reality-consciousness-bliss (*sat-chit-ānanda*). It no longer requires rebirth.

What has been described is *Raja* ("royal") *Yoga*, as outlined by Patanjali, with all its eight limbs. It is important to keep this in mind because the usual connotation of *yoga* in the West is confined to the first two limbs, particularly to the *āsanas*. A popular television program equates yoga virtually in entirety with various physical exercises.

Well over 250 such postures can be identified, and there is an elaborate literature on methods of cleansing internal organs, for example, the methods advised by Vyas Dev:

> Before sitting in deep meditation for a long time ... the yogi should clear his bowels completely by drawing in and expelling water through his anus, empty his bladder by drawing in water and then expelling it through a catheter, and purify his digestive system by swallowing and extracting about seventy feet of string made of fine yarn. He should also swallow two or three pints of lukewarm salt water to make himself vomit and swallow and extract a three-inch-wide strip of cloth seven yards long to finish the job. Then he is ready for serious meditation.[15]

Patanjali, himself, however, was not nearly so rigorous. For him, purification was to be practiced only to the extent necessary to get on with the main business of yoga, the remaining limbs after the first two have been completed.

There are yoga centers in America (e.g., the Kripalu Center in eastern Pennsylvania) that have integrated yoga practices with a wholistic approach to life, applying such concentration techniques to everyday life, cutting grass, printing a paper, and baking bread.

Yoga as taught by Patanjali, however, is an intense and long-range training. When one is advanced, it is possible to develop certain powers ordinarily thought of as supernatural. The yogin can still hunger and thirst, practice telepathy and clairvoyance, and possibly even retrieve knowledge of previous lives. But these powers are snares, since they are so readily used for selfish ends. The yogin is urged to give them up, and for that reason, the supernatural powers associated with yoga are rarely seen, certainly not photographed. As Swami Akhilananda used to insist, anyone who has such powers in a genuine spiritual quest will never display them or show them off. You can be certain, the swami maintained, that anyone who makes such claims cannot be genuine.

Gaining supernatural power is not the goal; it is a by-product on the way to *samādhi*. Serious yoga practice begins with access concentration, careful attention to one symbol, perhaps *OM*, perhaps even, as Akhilananda often prescribed, the Madonna Mary. When a mental identity with the primary object has been attained, one can move to the first *jhana*, identify without awareness of anything else. After this even the thought of awareness itself is to be obliterated, and all sense of duality is eliminated. Sri Ramakrishna focused at length on the figure of Mother Kālī and eventually came to feel united with her. Then, in a striking description of ecstasy, all feeling of self, Kālī, or any surroundings vanished. Words failed him in attempting to describe what he called Pure Bliss.

The final *samādhi* comes only when such a state can be extended into the normal realm of wakeful living in this world. When one can live in the state of pure bliss and carry on in the midst of his daily round of activities, he has become a *jivan-mukti* ("a liberated person"). This state is the "eternal present" in which personal consciousness is transcended permanently. For such a person there is neither ego nor world nor other persons. The broken unity has been restored. Ramakrishna's biographer described it thus:

> he is devoid of ideas of "I" and "mine," he looks on the body as a mere shadow, an outer sheath encasing the soul. He does not dwell on the past, takes no thought for the future, and looks with indifference on the present. He surveys everything in the world with an eye of equality; he is no longer touched by the infinite variety of phenomenon; he no longer reacts to pleasure and pain. He remains unmoved where he — that is to say, his body — is worshipped by the good or tormented by the wicked, for he realizes that it is the one Brahman that manifests itself through everything.[16]

Obviously, very little of this can be photographed. Dr. John Clark of Manchester, however, has attempted to portray it graphically, casting it in modern terms, using the model of a computer flow chart.[17]

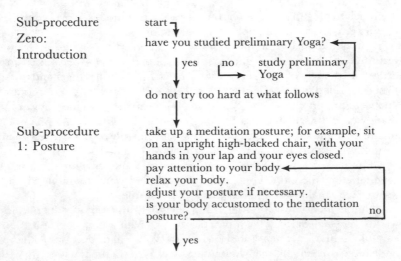

Sub-procedure Zero: Introduction

start
have you studied preliminary Yoga?
yes   no   study preliminary Yoga
do not try too hard at what follows

Sub-procedure 1: Posture

take up a meditation posture; for example, sit on an upright high-backed chair, with your hands in your lap and your eyes closed.
pay attention to your body
relax your body.
adjust your posture if necessary.
is your body accustomed to the meditation posture?   no
yes

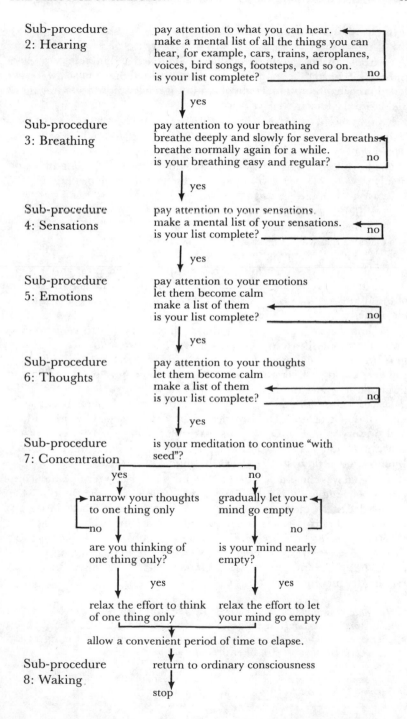

Sub-procedure 2: Hearing — pay attention to what you can hear. make a mental list of all the things you can hear, for example, cars, trains, aeroplanes, voices, bird songs, footsteps, and so on. is your list complete? — no

yes

Sub-procedure 3: Breathing — pay attention to your breathing breathe deeply and slowly for several breaths breathe normally again for a while. is your breathing easy and regular? — no

yes

Sub-procedure 4: Sensations — pay attention to your sensations. make a mental list of your sensations. is your list complete? — no

yes

Sub-procedure 5: Emotions — pay attention to your emotions let them become calm make a list of them is your list complete? — no

yes

Sub-procedure 6: Thoughts — pay attention to your thoughts let them become calm make a list of them is your list complete? — no

yes

Sub-procedure 7: Concentration — is your meditation to continue "with seed"?

yes — narrow your thoughts to one thing only — no

no — gradually let your mind go empty — no

are you thinking of one thing only?

is your mind nearly empty?

yes — relax the effort to think of one thing only

yes — relax the effort to let your mind go empty

allow a convenient period of time to elapse.

Sub-procedure 8: Waking — return to ordinary consciousness

stop

The Dhamma of the Buddha

Buddhism, the lengthened shadow of Siddhartha Gautama, who later came to be called "The Buddha" (lit., the enlighted óne, or the awakened one), has been the spiritual light of Asia. It is now rapidly becoming more and more popular in the West.

Roughy twenty-five hundred years ago, Prince Siddhartha was being trained for his royal inheritance, when — so the legends tell us — he saw an old man, a sick man, and a dead man, followed by a recluse whose example he followed. He tried various ascetic practices for a long time and finally gave them up in favor of an enlightenment which he taught in the Four Aryan ("noble") truths.

1. Suffering (*dukkha*) exists
2. Suffering is the result of *taṇha* ("clinging")
3. There is a way of release from *dukkha*, and it is
4. The Noble Eightfold Path.

We alluded to this Eightfold Path in the previous chapter, and it is not within the scope of this guide to develop in any detail the magnificent life of the Buddha. Our task is to look at the spiritual practices developed in his name.[18]

We know very little about Buddhism during its first three centuries, until the time of Emperor Aśoka, who gave it royal patronage and sent missionaries throughout southeast Asia, especially to what we now call Sri Lanka. A body of literature in the Pāli language developed and spread throughout South and Southeast Asia. The literature was known as the *Tipitika* (or *Tripitika*), literally meaning "three baskets" (of palm leaf documents). The teachings and practice of the Path outlined by the Buddha and preserved in Pāli documents was called *Theravāda* (the Way of the Elders), although this is only one of the many schools of "Hinayāna" Buddhism that flourished in the early Buddhist centuries.

The goal was the practice of the Buddha's *dhamma*, a term that encompasses teaching and practice, the way of life taught by the Buddha. The *dhamma* led many men, and some women, to seek arahantship, the state of the liberated person who has conquered *taṇha* by means of a disciplined practice of the eightfold path. The *bhikkhus* ("monks," lit. beggars) and a few *bhikkhunis* ("nuns") practiced lives of discipline, focusing on meditation. They took refuge in the Triple Gem, the Three Jewels of Buddhism, reciting frequently,

> *Buddhaṁ saraṇaṁ gacchāmi* (I take refuge in the Buddha)
> *Dhammaṁ saraṇaṁ gacchāmi* (I take refuge in the dhamma)
> *Saṅghaṁ saraṇaṁ gacchāmi* (I take refuge in the saṅgha, the congregation or the fellowship of likeminded people).*

---

*Monks chanting this triple jewel can be seen and heard briefly in some films, *Buddhism: Be Ye Lamps Unto Yourselves* and *Buddhism: The Path to Enlightenment*.

In the Theravāda tradition, there is a variety of approaches, but all of them are means of what might be called relaxed intensity to attain to a state of insight and mindfulnss, Right Seeing. Terms like *vipassana* ("insight") and *satipaṭṭhāna* ("mindfulness") are used. Two important manuals have appeared, the *Satipaṭṭhāna Sūtta* and the *Visuddhimagga*.[19] Both stress the importance of virtue (*sīla*), as we have seen. The *Satipaṭṭhāna Sūtta* then goes on to describe the basic observation, breath.

> And how, monks, does a monk dwell practicing body contemplation and the body?
> Herein, monks, a monk having gone to the forest, to the foot of a tree, or to an empty place, sits down crosslegged, keeps his body erect and his mindfulness alert. Just mindful he breathes in and mindful he breathes out.
> Breathing in a long breath, he knows I am breathing in a long breath ... (and so on)

What comes more naturally than breath? But how little attention is paid to this vital life process!

Some forms of yoga prescribe elaborate breath exercises in which one is taught to control the flow of air in and out, in one nostril out another, held for lengths of time, and so on. By contrast, most Buddhist schools teach breath awareness rather than breath control. If one simply becomes aware of breathing, either by concentrating on the sensation of air entering and leaving the nostrils or by feeling the sensation of a rising and falling abdomen, changes in breathing patterns do occur. Like posture, breath observation assists one to lose consciousness of the illusion called self.

Nyanaponika insists that breathing is an exercise in mindfulness, it is not a breathing exercise. Since breath is always with us, Nyanaponika urges that we turn our attention to it whenever there is a free moment. It quiets the body, and hence also the mind, and makes attention much more possible. Just as posture awareness can focus the whole self so can breath awareness. Indeed few practices are equal to simply breath awareness in teaching impermanence (*anicca*), and certainly no lecture or book will do as well.

Breath observation is the first step on the ladder of mindfulness, the beginning of "bare attention," the single-minded awareness of what is actually happening to us and in us. Normally we do not pay attention to what our senses register, but we judge each sensation from the vantage point of our own self-interest. Bare attention allows each impression to speak for itself, giving the meditator freedom to act without the urge to do "something" at any cost. Bare attention is the exact opposite of daydreaming, which fantasizes an imagined past and a contemplated future.

Bare attention is followed by clear comprehension wherein what has been experienced in bare attention is related to goals. Commentaries distinguish four kinds of clear comprehension: (1) of purpose, (2) of suitability, (3) of the domain of meditation, and (4) of reality. The first two are easy enough to understand, although they may be difficult to practice. To relate everything to the domain of meditation, however, is to maintain a mindful attitude all the time so that all activities are ultimately parts of the meditative process. That is, meditation is no longer confined to times of disciplined sitting, but it becomes the controlling attitude of all of life. To relate experiences to reality requires the realization of the Theravāda's most important insight: "*Within* there is no self that acts, and *outside* there is no self affected by the action."[20] This statement is not a doctrine to be taught; the first step toward its realization is simple concentration on the breath.

Having calmed and trained the mind in this fashion, attention can then be turned to the four objects of meditation: the body, feeling, state of mind, and mental contents. In the life of the bhikkhu, even contemplation on the body can be intense. In advanced stages, for example, it might involve close attention to a decomposing corpse. "Verily, this body of mine, too, is of the same nature as that body, it will become like that, and will not escape it."[21] Feelings and states of mind when unexamined determine the course of our actions. When carefully observed, however, they, like breath, become a part of the meditative process. They can then lead to the culture and development of the mind. Nyanaponika concludes,

> ...Satipaṭṭhāna does not require any elaborate *technique* or external devices. The daily life is its working material. It has nothing to do with any exotic cults or rites nor does it confer "initiations" or "esoteric knowledge" in any way other than by self-enlightenment.[22]

This statement will not be true of all systems of meditation, but it is important in understanding the Theravāda.*

In the early centuries of Buddhist life, another interpretation developed as well, called the *Mahāyāna* ("the great vehicle"), with a vast body of Sanskrit literature that spread, in translation, throughout all of northern Asia, including particularly China and Japan. The Mahāyāna did not repudiate the Theravāda (nor, as some manuals would have it, supersede it), but it added the image of the *bodhisattva*. Originally *bodhisattva* meant Gautama before his birth as the Buddha-to-be and then one who would vow to assist others in the journey to salvation. Later Mahāyānism saw bodhisattvas as beings of infinite compassion, looking out in mercy on all. The most important bodhisattva is Avalokiteśvara, whose eyes can be seen on the stupa-temples in Kathmandu, looking out in mercy and helpfulness over the whole valley. Avalokiteśvara was carried into China and Japan where "he" came to be regarded as a female figure, Kwan-yin of Kwannon.

---

*Fortunately, there are some good films on the Theravāda. They cover much more ground than spiritual practices, but they will be useful after the necessary preparation has been accomplished. See the discussion of films we have already mentioned in this chapter.

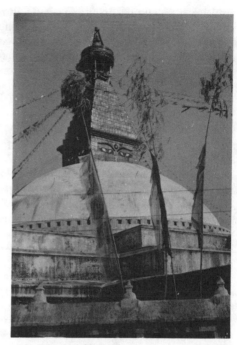

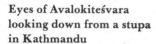

Eyes of Avalokiteśvara
looking down from a stupa
in Kathmandu

The Mahāyāṇa developed a vast amount of literature, beginning with wisdom books, the *Prājñapāramītāsūtras*, and climaxing in what is perhaps the most important piece of Mahāyāṇa literature, the Lotus Scripture. Called in Sanskrit the *Saddharmapuṇḍarikasūtra* ("Book about the Lotus of the True Law or way of life"). The Lotus Sutra was later translated into Chinese and then used in Japan under the name *Myōhō Renge Kyō* ("Book about the Lotus of the Mysterious Way"). Both these books became important in Mahāyāṇa spiritual practices, and it is important to note that as Buddhism went from place to place it changed, sometimes quite dramatically, an illustration in itself of a basic Buddhist doctrine of *anicca*, that there is nothing permanent or everlasting — not even the Buddhist religion itself.

The Mahāyāṇa developed an amazing variety of traditions, with their own spiritual practices. Their Japanese forms may be the easiest to understand. With spiritual practices centering around the use of the Lotus Scripture and other important verbal formulae, frequently including veneration of departed relatives, there developed various forms of esoteric Buddhism, including The True Word sects, Shingon and Tendai. Far more popular were the forms of piety directed toward Buddha Amida (*Amithaba* in Sanskrit and *O-mi-to* in Chinese).

By this time, the figure of Gautama had receded into the background of Mahāyāṇa thinking as a *Manushi Buddha* ("one who had done his work") and the *Dhyani Buddhas* ("Buddhas to be contemplated") became more prominent. The most prominent is Amida, who will save his devotees by taking them to a western paradise where life will be much more conducive to spiritual development than conditions in this world. These denominations — chiefly Jodo and Jodo-shin — use a formula, *Namu Amida Butsu* ("I adore the Buddha Amida").*

Influenced by both these schools and rejecting them vigorously was Nichiren who became politically involved during the Kamakura Shogunate (thirteenth century). He embraced the Lotus Scripture as "the key to everything." Instead of chanting *Namu Amida Butsu*, he prescribed the mantra *Namu Myōhō Renke Kyō*, venerating the Lotus Scripture instead of Amida. Nichiren sects splintered, and some came to be powerful. *Rissho Kosei Kai* has a strong influence in Japan, and *Nichiren Shoshu Sokagakkai* is now an important force all over the world.†

Meanwhile another form of the Mahāyāṇa was developing, destined to become increasingly popular in the West, particularly in the United States. The land of Tibet saw an unusual amalgamation of Theravāda, Mahāyāṇa and Tantric practices that uses material things to probe spiritual reality. What was said earlier about the *Satipaṭṭhāna Sutta* and the *Visuddhimagga* can apply in large measure to Tibetan meditative and spiritual practices. Their aims are not dissimilar, although the outward manifestations provide a vivid visual contrast. The most important contrast is the Tibetan stress on the bodhisattva, returning to the world to assist others on the path. A *lama* (Tibetan "priest") is a *tulku*, which means a reincarnation of a bodhisattva, and the chief religious officer, the Dalai Lama, is a reappearance of Avalokiteśvara himself. The Tibetan meditator begins with *sila* and proceeds to *samadhi*, fixing the mind on one point. But more elaborate instructions and techniques are available to the adept. The Tibetan Book of the Dead, the Book of the Great Liberation, and the Teachings of Milarepa are basic texts in this system of thought,†† but the Tibetan way has become influential in America largely under the influence of Chogyam Trungpa Rimpoche.‡

In addition to films on Tibet, instructors can find good reproductions of the Wheel of Life, virtually a picture of the whole universe as seen from the Tibetan point of view. The outer rim of the wheel contains the twelve links in the chain of interdependent causation. This is a chain of *saṃsāra*: birth, suffering, death, and rebirth. Beginning with ignorance as the root cause of all life-death processes (top right of the outer rim) actions are produced. The accumulation of actions results in consciousness, which is

*Unfortunately, good film coverage of True Word and Pure Land Buddhism is hard to find. *Buddhism: Land of the Disappearing Buddha* presents an adequate description of Japanese piety, featuring Pure Landism, but it shows little in the way of Pure Land spiritual practices.

†*Buddhism: Land of the Disappearing Buddha* has some striking footage of this sect, including their headquarters at the foot of Mount Fuji. See also films produced by, and primarily for, the Nichiren Shoshu Academy.

††See bibliography.

‡*Requiem for a Faith* is a sensitive treatment of Tibetan Buddhism, but it shows little of the depth of Tibetan spiritual practice. For a more adequate treatment, see *Prophecy*, the first film in *Tibetan Trilogy*.

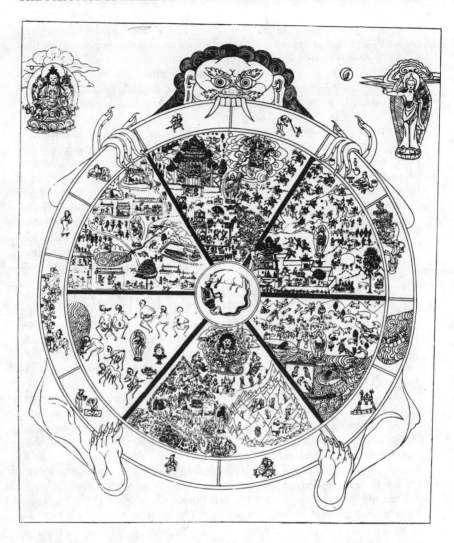

The Wheel of Life (Tibetan)
from L. Austine Waddell, *Tibetan Buddhism* (London: W. H. Allen & Co., 1895. Dover Reprint, 1972)

finally projected into the realm of time and space. This is rebirth, the projection of consciousness into name and form (*nama rupa*). Immediately the senses begin to operate, making contact with the world, producing sensations which result in desire, which produces in turn the most dangerous item in the circle, clinging or grasping (*tanha*). Grasping results in becoming, then birth, then of course, death, with the circle continuing on and on.

The inner, larger, area shows five "destinations," or states of beings: the realm of the gods (upper left) and the realm of humans (upper right). There is also the realm of animals, the land of the hungry ghosts (insatiable appetites), and the hells. None of these conditions is permanent. They are ways by which one who clings to him/her self perceives the world. The motivating force is seen in the three animals in the hub: the rooster of passion, the snake of malice, and the pig of ignorance. In the upper right the Buddha points to texts describing the way out of this endless repetition. Ignoring many of the rich details in this psychocosmogram, we note only that it is all in the jaws of illusion, and when one comes to enlightenment, it will be swallowed up and cease to exist.[23]

Zen is another popular Buddhist school of spiritual practices. It became popular in America largely through the efforts of Daisetz T. Suzuki, although there are now many Zen centers of all kinds throughout the country. With a Mahāyāṇa flavor derived from Japan, the spiritual practices of Zen are more akin to the Theravāda, and it is not too wide of the mark to say that its practices are those of the Theravāda combined with a rigorous Japanese precision.*

Zen came to Japan through the efforts of Bodhidharma, who refined its Chinese form. The word *zen* is a cognate of the Sanskrit *dhyana*, which simply means "meditation." The different schools, Rinzai, Sōtō, and Ōbaku being the chief ones, need not concern us at this time. We shall concentrate on the Sōtō school.†

A manual for Sōtō Zen practice maintains that *zazen* ("the practice of Zen") is the gateway to the heart of Buddhism. "Whoever practices Zazen with his whole mind and body is himself Buddha for the light within him is the original light of Buddha Sakyamuni." The three jewels and the bodhisattva doctrine are present as well. At the So-ji-ji Temple in Kamakura the day begins at 4:00 a.m. and contains three sessions of zazen sitting, totaling at least five hours, plus two services and two hours of cleaning and working. Zazen can be seen as a refinement of the practices seen earlier in this chapter, but with detailed instructions. For example,

the most important thing is a straight back and the base of the spine should be straightened as soon as the legs are comfortably settled. Breathe easily through the nose with the belly steady and lean

---

*Two films mentioned before are useful here: *Buddhism: Land of the Disappearing Buddha* and *Zen in Ryoku-in*.

†Some of the following material is drawn from a delightful pamphlet prepared for visitors to the So-Ji-ji Temple in Yokohama.

neither to the left nor to the right. Sway the body slightly from left to right with the movements getting progressively smaller and then sit steadily and quietly, with your left hand on your right palm and the thumbs touching each other. Keep the eyes open during Zazen although not too widely so and keep the breathing steady. The eyes must be fixed on one point about three metres away. Do not try to think and do not try not to think: just sit with your mind bright. Here I must utter a word of warning. Do NOT think of Enlightenment nor of becoming Buddha — such thoughts retard progress. Simply carry on sitting quietly and patiently with a truly repentant heart and your True Mind will show itself suddenly so that you will be filled with a peace and joy that are indescribable — suddenly the old world will be eternally new and everything in it will be of the essence of Buddha. It is an impossibility to describe the experience — the reader must gain his own for himself.

However, Zen for all its precision is not mechanical. This intense concentration, coupled with a highly developed aesthetic sense,* and the

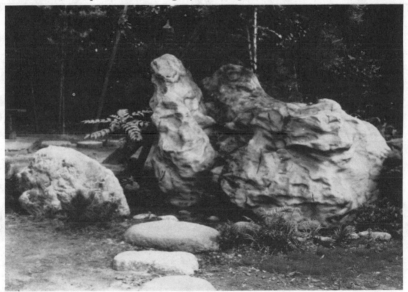

Garden in a Japanese home

use of insoluble riddles called *koans* are highly effective means of ridding the meditator of a clinging to his or her own ego. Aesthetic practices related to Zen are many, including gardening and the tea ceremony.†

*All the films dealing with Zen will illustrate this.
†The tea ceremony is beautifully described in *The Path*, but it is important to consult Part II of this book before using this film in a classroom.

In the film *Buddhism: Land of the Disappearing Buddha* students may question the beating administered twice in the films depicting Zen meditation, and a word of explanation is in order. The stick carried by the Zen master is called a *kyosaku*, and the manual prepared for visitors to the Jo-Ji-ji Temple has the following statement.

> *Kyosaku.* Do not be disturbed by any sounds you may hear and do not be surprised if you are struck with the kyosaku. Remember that pain is based on fear, and surprise is based on fear, and both are forms of thinking. Apart from the obvious uses of the kyosaku which are: 1. to wake up those who fall asleep and 2. to teach those who move that it is unwise to do so for they must keep the correct posture . . . the kyosaku is of great value in proving whether or not a meditation is genuine. In this connection I quote the following from the Dhammapada, "Even as a rock is unshaken by the wind, so are the wise unmoved by praise or blame." This may seem a strange use of the above quotation but a little thought and some experience of the kyosaku will bring out my meaning quite fully. Remember that, when one is beyond the opposites praise and blame, reward and punishment, are the same thing, and welcome the kyosaku when it is administered as something of great value. It is an impossibility for me to explain what I am trying to say but I can assure the reader that, when used properly, the kyosaku is of inestimable value, for it can cut through our illusions in a way that nothing else can and it can strengthen us in our resolve. It is also useful as a test of how well we have rooted out our passions; for instance, if we feel anger when struck we are not yet truly empty of hate. There are many other uses of the kyosaku which will become apparent to individual people for it fits individual cases perfectly. Remember that it is both a reward and a punishment and that we are sitting in Zazen in order to become men and women of iron while being completely at peace within.

Little wonder that Zen is useful for the training of soldiers and policemen.

CHAPTER 3

Sound and Motion

TWO APPROACHES divide academic studies of religion into opposing camps. Those disciplines that prescribe precision and externally imposed order purvey an identifiable body of knowledge consisting of doctrines, dogmas, and intellectual ideas to be mastered (and tested and graded). But more basic is human experience itself. To stand aside and allow centuries of it to speak to us is difficult, for the data is not orderly, and we cannot simply stand outside and observe.

Questions about God or the gods, and similar theological questions, then, are less important than they appear at first glance. Even attempts to validate truth claims of the various religious traditions recede into insignificance, for the "truth" of a religion may not be demonstrable by methods philosophers used to call a theory of correspondence. The truth of a religion may be in its ability to inspire true living, for in the traditions we are dealing with here, a search for the truth is less important than the truth of the search. Religious commitment and religious community do not necessarily require "belief" in God, per se.

In this light precise doctrines, dogmas, and creeds are the least likely vehicle for sharing a religious experience. College courses on Hindu or Buddhist phenomena that deal only with an intellectual expression are wide of the mark.

In the Beginning — Word

Most western students are familiar with the opening words of the Gospel According to John in the New Testament, where *word* (*logos*) precedes creation. "All things were made through [the *logos*] and without him was not anything made that was made" (John 1:3). Before exploring the Hindu counterpart of this statement, we turn our attention to the Gospel of John itself.

With his satanic dog at his feet, Goethe's Faust turned for comfort to the New Testament, attempting to translate "the holy original in [his] beloved German." He turned appropriately enough to the opening words of this Gospel: "im Anfang war das Wort!" ("In the beginning was the word.") But there he stopped short. *Wort* was inadequate to render *logos*. And so he struggled:

Wenn ich vom Geiste recht erleuchtet bin
Geschrieben steht: im Anfant war der Sinn.
(If I have been rightly taught by the Spirit, the writing would be,
"In the beginning was the *Thought!*")

This version too cannot satisfy, and he tries again.

... im Anfang war die *Kraft!*" ("Power")

Closer perhaps, but not close enough.

... im Anfang war die *That!*" ("Deed")

at which time the dog Mephistopheles in disguise — begins to growl.

In choosing *deed* over *word* Faust simply confirmed the original meaning of *word*, for words are deeds. If I so much as say "Good morning," I must emerge from my isolation, place myself before someone, and allow some portion of my power to pass to him or her for good or for ill. If I withhold my "Good morning," I withhold my potency. So Faust concludes "I cannot the mere word so highly prize." To utter words is to set power in motion. Religion — often seen as a response to power — uses words. No wonder that in the Buddhist eightfold path the first specific exhortation following the demand for right seeing and right aspirations is to control the tongue: Right Speaking.

Some words are written; some are spoken; some are chanted; some are mumbled. But even when they are used to express a set of ideas, the intellectual expression of religious experience, they connote more by suggestion than they denote by definition. As a community becomes more and more "civilized," written language tends to be given greater and greater prominence.

Numinous Sounds

I enjoyed putting together a tape-recording of familiar sounds to play to a class assembled in New York. First there was a bell, sonorous and clear (actually from a Baltimore fire engine). Then the same bell rang with agitation, and it could be recognized as a symbol of alarm. This was followed by deep-toned and then high-pitched temple bells from Japan. There was a *shofar* as blown on the Jewish High Holy Days, followed by a lallation, an eerie sound made by women at a Hindu wedding in Calcutta, followed by a funeral wail by Toda women. Lastly there was an ambulance siren whining on New York's Sixth Avenue. Each of these sounds produced an instant response.

But what had we heard? First of all there were disturbances in the air as a bell rang or a whistle blew. These waves vibrated the diaphragm of a sensitive microphone which in turn set up a series of electrical pulsations carried by two wires into a portable Uher. There they were manipulated by a series of transistors and additional power added to energize a magnet that in turn altered the pattern of magnetism on a piece of plastic tape. The day I played those sounds for my class, another magnet reversed this process, and additional electrical power was added in a pattern influenced by the succession of magnetic impulses on the tape, to energize a loud-speaker cone, which in turn disturbed the air currents in the classroom, producing a vibration on all the eardrums in the room (and possibly beyond), which in turn created electrical disturbances in nerves causing a "sound" to register somewhere in the brain.

Nothing — literally *no thing* — passed from one medium to another, and the only sound that existed was the "sound" experience of the hearer. We are accustomed to the old question, if a tree falls in the forest and there is no one to hear it, did it make a sound? The answer, of course, depends on one's definition of *sound*. From our point of view there is none. But what if there had been no disturbance of the air, and yet the sound had been heard with equal clarity? Sound in this case can be experienced, even though no air-disturbance reached an ear.

We may start with air and vibrations in breath which is the support of life itself. Breath shapes itself into sounds. And so Genesis I has God creating the universe by his breath, and the Fourth Gospel begins, "In the beginning was the word (*Logos*: Heb. *Debir*) . . . and the word was with God and the word was God." Obviously *logos* and *debir* do not refer merely to syllables or letters. But syllables and letters are involved. Compare this understanding with a Tantric text.

> *Prajāpatir vai idam āsīt* (In the beginning was Brahman.)
> *Tasya vāg avitīyā āsīt* (With whom was Vāk or the Word)
> She is spoken of as second to Him because she is first potentially in and then as Śakti issues from Him
> *Vāg vai paramam Brahma* (And the word is Brahman)
> *Vāk* is thus a *Śakti* or Power of the Brahman.[24]

Breath in Sanskrit is *prāna*, and *prāna* is what gives life, just as in Hebrew life comes from *nefesh*, which also means "breath." In Hindu thought this breath is shaped into the mystic syllable *Om*. Such a sound develops a life of its own, and sounds, rhythms and the like, have a definite effect on the human psyche. From this develops the phenomenon of *mantra*, a set of syllables that, when recited correctly — even if recited only to oneself with no audible sound — produces an effect.

In the presence of numinous phenomena — experiences that arouse in us a spirit of awe — we tend to respond in nonintelligible syllables. If the sounds can actually be translated into ordinary speech, the translation is unimportant, for a translated mantra is no mantra at all. *Namu myōhō renge kyō* translates into "I adore the Lotus Sutra," but that isn't what it means at all. These spoken words have power, and the power is in the mantra itself. The Latin term is *carmen* from which we get the English word *charm*. Originally a charm was not an object; it was a word or a succession of words. You, therefore, need counter charms to offset evil effects of having unleashed power by reciting a powerful name. "Thou shalt not invoke the name of Yahweh thy God to evil intent" is a fair rendering of the commandment in Deuteronomy 5, so a devout Jew, if he even mentions the word *God*, follows it with the counter charm, "Blessed be He," and a devout Muslim, if he mentions the Prophet (Muḥammad) follows it with a similar phrase.

In the presence of something unusual it is common to respond with words that connote either deity or the early form in which deity was appropriated, sexuality. To invoke the name of God in such a situation is not at all a prayer, it is the unconscious attempt to counteract power with another power, the power of a potent spoken word. Sexual terms are similarly used, and some people are excited by the use of certain sexual terms, and others are repulsed. Few are neutral. Also, there is the well-known tendency to avoid speaking of possible disaster, lest one bring it on.

Written words, never as powerful as spoken words, are fetishes, and writing is a form of magic. Some Kabbalists insist that when God created the world he did so out of the letters of the Hebrew alphabet. "And God said, let there be ... and there was." What he said was in the Hebrew language.

The chant, the dance, the exorcism, then, combine movement and sound so as to evoke and to control power. Whatever external effect they may have, their ability to arouse an intense effect on devotees is evident. Few western art forms approach the grandeur of a well-choreographed high mass.*

---

*The available films are of little direct value here, even though almost all of them contain some elements of sound and motion. When viewers are alerted to this aspect, careful attention to sounds and movements will be valuable in using virtually any film.

CHAPTER 4

Contrasting Paradigms

MANY SPIRITUAL practices, including meditation, can be used in connection with almost any ontological understanding, or none at all. Quiet sitting and attention to breathing does not require commitment to the doctrine of *anatta* ("no self"). Nonetheless, some points of view are more compatible with spiritual practices than others, and if a course of instruction is intended to open the doors of spiritual perception in Hindu and Buddhist contexts, the practices must be seen as the visible side of a commitment to Ultimate Reality that is quite different from the usual viewpoint of the West.

It is no more difficult, however, to understand the theoretical basis of a Hindu or Buddhist worldview than it is to study quantum physics. Indeed, there is a remarkable similarity between the two insights into the nature of reality. Physicists are as quick as spiritual leaders to tell us that our ordinary way of looking at the world is not Right Seeing. Without a change in our ordinary perception, quantum theory and thermodynamics will be incomprehensible. When it is understood that $E = MC^2$, and when the intricate relationship between matter and energy and the relativity of time is appreciated, atomic science and modern technology can be pursued. What a shame to teach scientific Right Seeing in our universities and couple it with religious naiveté. Is it any wonder that technology that ought to serve human ends threatens to destroy humanity?[25]

This chapter will explore contrasting world views, but first a sharply stated contrast, overdrawn only in that it is a typology which does not describe all members of either set. Great souls (*mahātmas*) have developed in every culture.

> Western man tends to seek for deity beyond the self and the world; for man in the East, the search for divinity is ultimately a search within. "The only Buddha," the Buddhists can say, "is the Buddha which is found within one's own heart ... The one view leads to an underlying calm, to an assumption of innocence and a rejection of notions of "responsibility"; the other leads to anxiety, to concepts of freedom, concern, and guilt. The one world, reflecting protective — maternal — psycho-spiritual norms, insists upon the validity of the inward journey; the other with an aggressive — paternal — bent insists upon the validity of thrust and outer conquest. The meeting of East and West is an ideal which may be valid as a guide to action. It is inconceivable on the profound levels of belief.[26]

From the Parts to the Whole

We can contrast two opposing viewpoints. One of them is called by Erich Fromm "the being" mode. The second is called the "having" mode. In this mode we possess nature and the world, and we identify ourselves in terms of how much we possess. Individual selves become superior not only to the planet but to other individual selves, and a hierarchy is set up. Living East of Eden, our primal unity destroyed, we live in an adversary relationship with the world, and with almost everybody in it.

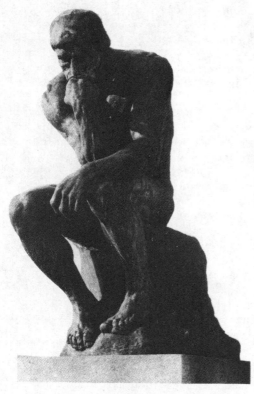

Auguste Rodin, The Thinker, bronze ca. 1880. Courtesy of the Cleveland Museum of Art. Gift of Ralph King

Rodin's famous sculpture, The Thinker, shows the predicament of modern man brought up in this milieu. Originally conceived as part of a larger work called "The Gates of Hell," the figure is thinking, not at all meditating. Notice the tenseness in every muscle. Here is judgment, reward, punishment. Here is fear of experience and terror at certain sensations. Here is the relegation of half the world to the realm of darkness, not to be seen, not to be trafficked with.

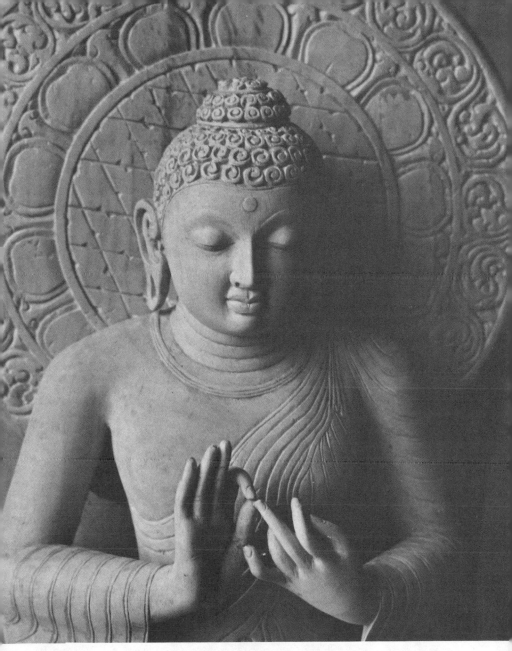

Japanese image of the Buddha

From the Whole to the Parts

If Rodin's tense man is the thinker of the West, the Buddha is the thinker of the East, but there is a vast difference in what he thinks. In place of an

adversarial relation, there is the realization that between myself and the cosmos, between myself and other selves, between myself and God there is no real distance. Not because I am God nor because I am the world, but because the entity I had thought of as "I" has meaning only in terms of the whole.

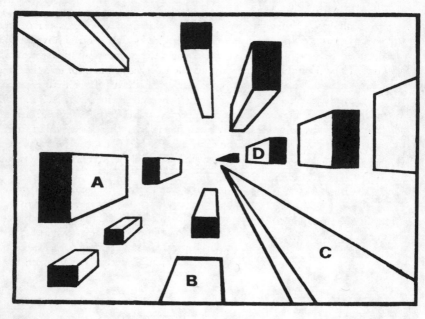

A popular book on Tantra uses this illustration of what the author calls "the everyday view of time and history." This illustration is supposed to represent something of the way the world looks through the rear view mirror of an automobile.

Objects appear out of an invisible future within our field of vision, framed in our "present moment," which defines our immediate sense-experience and knowledge. As time goes by things, as they get older, seem to recede towards the horizon. All things seem as though they must have beginnings and ends. A is a person we have known all our lives who has died. We can "see" his life entire from beginning to end. Other people and things, like B, have begun and are still with us. Some existed, like D, far back in history. Others, like the earth, at C, may seem to have been always there. But our astronomy suggests that in this kind of time the world may have had an infinitely remote beginning, at the central vanishing point of our view of all things. Once, perhaps, when the world began, the frame of the present moment was at the central point, and all the later boxes in the frame are linked to each other by chains of cause and effect.[27]

Essentially such a viewpoint comes from viewing the cosmos as a carefully constructed edifice of small building blocks. Most of us have been conditioned to see the world as consisting of innumerable parts, atoms that used to be thought of as the indivisible unit of matter, put together to form larger parts, in turn assembled into still larger units. The universe, then, is simply a collection of parts, each discrete in its individual existence, and an order must be maintained by some kind of authoritative scheme. This viewpoint inevitably leads to my desire to be central in such an organization, at the peak of the hierarchy, and the fact that many western religions condemn pride as a cardinal sin is only a further testimony to the full acceptance of this viewpoint.

On the basis of our past recollections we may try to predict the future (E) before it breaks into our field of vision. In this fragmented view of things, each of us has his separate mirror, but where is the self looking at "things." Individual things have reality here. The author uses another illustration which will seem more fanciful at first. Here all the things we thought we saw in the rear view mirror are actually projected from the mouth of the present.

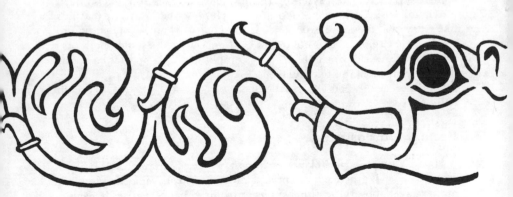

Here again there is a sequence of events and a linear presentation of things, but the real difference is that we realize in this diagram that each individual's perception of things and events are being expelled from one's own consciousness, the mouth of the monster that has taken the place of the mirror in the previous figure.

We will never be able to find the origin or causes of all things "out there," among older projected things. Their origin is in the projection-mechanism itself, that is to say, within the psycho-physical organism. And what is being projected is the tissue of experience and memory we call reality. It is part of the mechanism's function to make reality seem solid, spread out around us and looking as if it must have had a beginning far back in time.[28]

If this monster is turned around and we look into its mouth, we have the figure of the Wheel of Life, shown on page 25. Meditation on the Wheel of Life and on the Hindu Śrī Cakra serve similar ends.

Experience and Doctrine

A mystical experience is not the same as mysticism, or a mystical doctrine. The experience is a moment of immediate awareness, and it takes place all over the world. Muḥammad experienced it on the Night of Power and Excellence when the angel Gabriel appeared to him and began revealing the Qur'ān. The Buddha knew it under his Bodhi tree. Paul was struck blind on the road to Damascus, and Ramakrishna experienced ecstatic union with Mother Kālī.

Mystical theology, however, is something else. Although Paul had a vivid experience, and Isaiah went into a trance state in the Temple, Isaiah did not try to instruct King Ahab on how to experience the presence of God, and Paul specifically cautioned the Corinthians against seeking ecstasy. The Buddha, however, and even more so Ramakrishna or Caitanya built religious systems around the experience and, like some of the upaniṣads, made instruction in the techniques central. For teachers like Caitanya, then, the experience is the goal. It is not a way-station to somewhere else. Reality is not in some other realm to be sought at the expense of this world. Spiritual practices emphasize the importance of this present moment at this particular spot. As emphasized earlier, meditative practices are bodily acts at particular locations. Hence, the stress of breath and posture.

Breath and Posture

Hatha Yoga prescribes elaborate breath exercises and rigorous body exercises. Zazen is practiced with precise muscle control. Vipassana is much more relaxed, observing rather than controlling. In every case, however, close attention to the movement of the breath — in and out, in and out, up and down, up and down, inhale and exhale, inhale and exhale — renders teaching the doctrine superfluous. *Anatta* is experienced. A manual on Zen says,

When we inhale, the air comes into the inner world. When we exhale, the air goes out to the outer world. The inner world is limitless,

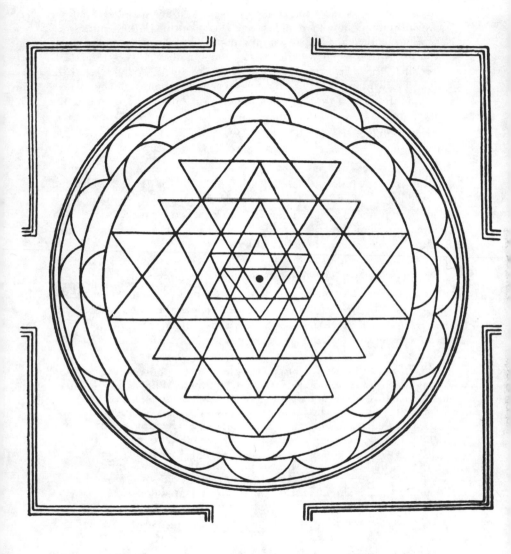

The Sri Cakra
from Ernst Lehner, *Symbols, Signs & Signets* New York: Dover Publications, 1950

and the outer world is also limitless. We say "inner world" or "outer world," but actually there is just one whole world. In this limitless world, our throat is like a swinging door. The air comes in and goes out like someone passing through a swinging door. If you think, "I breathe," the "I" is extra. There is no you to say "I." What we call "I" is just a swinging door which moves when we inhale and when we exhale. It just moves; that is all. When your mind is pure and calm enough to follow this movement, there is nothing; no "I," no world, no mind nor body; just a swinging door.[29]

Spiritual practice rarely asks one to "believe" anything, but to enter faithfully into the practice itself. The Buddha said "*Eho passika*," which can be roughly translated, "Come and try it out for yourself." Dogmatic theologies may ask one to accept "in faith" — a prostitution of the word *faith* — a statement for which there is no evidence. The practices described in this book urge involvement in a way of living. Beliefs will then take care of themselves. If in time a belief does not bear the scrutiny of what is observed in practice, it will wither; there is no need to renounce it.

Posture, then, is a means of attaining spirituality. No matter what the specifics, the body controls the mind as much as the mind controls the body. The Zen manual quoted above continues with the following description of the zazen posture:

When you sit in the full lotus position, your left foot is on your right thigh, and your right foot is on your left thigh. When we cross our legs like this, even though we have a right leg and a left leg, they have become one. The position expresses the oneness of duality: not two, and not one. This is the most important teaching: not two, and not one. Our body and mind are not two and not one. If you think your body and mind are two, that is wrong; if you think that they are one, that is also wrong. Our body and mind are both two *and* one. We usually think that if something is not one, it is more than one; if it is not singular, it is plural. But in actual experience, our life is not only plural, but also singular. Each one of us is both dependent and independent.[30]

At the beginning of the process one needs a teacher, but the guru needed at the beginning can be dangerous. To attach oneself to a charismatic person may block the path to immediate awareness if the clutching is too tight.*

A Contemporary Guru: Rajnish is one of the very few films useful to illustrate the concerns of this chapter.

The Tyranny of the Absolute

Consider the figure of Humpty Dumpty, who sat on a wall. Humpty was an egg, an age-old symbol of the unity of life, for in certain Hindu cosmogonies the whole cosmos was seen as the breaking apart of a cosmic egg. An egg on top of the wall, able to view both sides, not partisan. But Humpty Dumpty had a great fall. He became one-sided and shattered into many pieces, so much so that "all the king's horses and all the king's men" — whatever mighty power in the having mode of existence there might be — "couldn't put Humpty together again!" All the king's horses and all the king's men can't do it because they are themselves the symbols of divisiveness and alienation, power confronting other power, leading to further destruction and the alienation of those who cannot submit to the ruling authority, ecclesiastical or political.

The tyranny of absolutism hangs like a scimitar over much Western thinking. Political alliances unite nations in order to exclude others, and sectarian schisms in religion frequently arise over the definition of small points of doctrine. The world can then be conveniently divided into friend and foe.

If there is no God except Allah, and if Muḥammad is his final prophet, and if there are only two classes of people in the world, the submitters and the sinners, there can be only one right way. If "there is no other name under heaven [except Jesus] given among men by which we must be saved," as Acts 4:12 proclaims, the world can be easily divided between the saved and the damned. In such unqualified orthodoxy, individual experience, unless it conforms strictly to a predetermined pattern, is suspect, and the priestly tradition exists to preserve the truth as revealed in the past and to check the excesses of human imagination.

The prophets of Israel, now considered canonical, and even Muḥammad himself, were opposed in their own day because they insisted that their experience was indeed valid. In virtually every tradition — including those that are the subject of this volume at times — those who make extensive use of contemplative practices can be an embarrassment.

We began with a consideration of three paths, *jñāna, bhakti,* and *karma.* This very tripartite scheme suggests immediately that there is no one absolute way. If all the king's horses and all the king's men cannot force Humpty Dumpty together again, perhaps the contemplative way of allowing the healing powers of a total world to take their own course can be tried. Ira Progoff, who has developed an intensive meditation system particularly for westerners, begins one of his books in this fashion,

> I remember the saying
> Of the old wise man, Lao Tze:
> "Muddy water,
> Let stand
> Becomes clear."[31]

A Focus on Center and Circumference

As a boy scout I learned to box the compass, recognizing the four cardinal directions as north, east, south, and west. In studying symbol systems from Kabbalah to Tantra, a fifth dimension appeared. To north, east, south, and west was added the center: right here. What is the difference between these two easily-expressed apperceptions?

It is typical of many cultures to place themselves at the center of the world. The Kaaba in Mecca, Mount Zion, Tenri City, or the Nile Valley have all been central in some schemes of thought, and maps of "the world" that hang on my wall invariably place the United States in the center. The mythic, three-story world — heaven above, hell beneath, and the world of man in the center — conveys a sense of order and importance. Galileo's heresy was not really his blasphemy against God or the scriptures; what disturbed his opponents most was his attack on anthropocentrism. Man was no longer the absolute center of God's concern.

By adding the fifth dimension, however, the figure suddenly changes. Now there will be many centers, as there are many heres and nows. Meditative and spiritual practices attempt to bring us to the center, but each to his or her own center. Whether we sit in a lecture room or a concert hall, we have difficulty centering on here and now. Like a monkey hopping from branch to branch, the mind goes off in all directions, but the music doesn't stop, and the lecture continues. Because our minds were somewhere else — in an imaginary never-never land for the most part — we suddenly realize that we missed what we paid good money to hear.

But we must go further. If I really reach the center, it is not exclusive, and there may be no real center. An intriguing Buddhist metaphor is sometimes known as "Indra's Net."

In this metaphorical illustration of codependent origination, the universe is represented by a giant net. Glistening jewels, each with its own particular color, shape, and texture, are positioned at every intersection of the strands in the meshwork. Thus each jewel is connected to every other jewel, and reflects them all in its individuality. We have here a model of organic unity — of unity which enhances the individuality of all participants.[32]

Maṇḍala

The Sanskrit word *maṇḍala* simply means "circle," and the circle has been an important symbol, both conscious and unconscious in many lands and times. Diagrams and drawings that came to be called maṇḍalas were used throughout the world as aids to meditation and as a means of centering a personality. The City of Madurai in South India and the City of Kyōtō in Japan were both consciously laid out as maṇḍalas. In Kyōtō the Emperor's palace stands at the center; in Madurai, the temple to Mīnakṣī.

The fragmented world we see with our senses, then, is not the real world. The real world is a whole, and in varying degrees we find ourselves fragmented and torn apart. Ancient India developed visual patterns to express not an attachment to wholeness but a search for it. Tucci says "The history of Indian religion may be defined as one of a toilsome attempt to attain autoconsciousness. Blending it altogether in a *darśana*, a unity of vision."[33] Whereas the western psychoanalyst C. G. Jung saw maṇḍala patterns primarily as attempts to heal broken personalities,[34] in Indian meditative practices they may be seen as ways of viewing the world.

As a meditative device, the maṇḍala is a method of developing self-consciousness, not the consciousness of individual selves in isolation but of the cosmic Self, centered in individual selves. Words such as these are perhaps too confusing to stand without further explanation.

We have stressed the appreciation of Hindu and Buddhist experience of the unity, or at least the non-duality, of the world. If I can come to a knowledge of myself with reference to the cosmos, I am no longer the captive of my accumulated karma but the free author of my future. But who am I? In high school algebra we learn equations like this: $A + B = AB$ (or possibly C). But in other kinds of mathematics we can say: $A + B = B$. What, then, happened to A?

Whenever the set "A" is a member of the set "B," A can be separated from B and its individuality recognized fully, but A cannot be added to B, since it is already part of the set. For example, if "A" = "all dogs" and "B" = "all quadrupeds," we can distinguish dogs from other quadrupeds, and the reality of dogness is not lost at all. We could add other subsets, Dobermans, poodles, and collies. If we add A and B, that is, combine "dogs" with "quadrupeds," the term A has disappeared, but B (quadrupeds in this case) has not increased. Nothing new has been added, a unity has been restored, a separation and isolation ended.

In Indian thought we may let A represent my individual self and B the great Self. A is real enough. It functions. It can be seen and dealt with. But to think of myself as absolutely separate from the world or the great Self is deceptively partial seeing. A added to B does not aggrandize B, but it no longer distinguishes A. Concentration on a maṇḍala lets me realize my own potential in this same way. My center becomes one with the real center so that I am no longer isolated as a separate and separating ego. This liberation cannot be accomplished by any outside force, and even in Pure Land Buddhism, Amida ultimately only creates the conditions whereby the devotee can reach this realization.

The Form of the Maṇḍala

Reduced to its basic elements the maṇḍala has a center, lines, and circles. The center may be a *bindu* ("dot").

●

In the Sanskrit language *bindu* can mean a detached particle, a drop, a spot, or the dot over a letter, especially *m*, to produce a kind of humming sound. It has a variety of meanings, including the mark between the eyebrows or, as some lexicographers suggest, the marks made by a lover on the lips of his mistress.

Here, however, it connotes both everythingness and nothingness (every-thing-ness and no-thing-ness) and is often indistinguishable in psychic functions from the circle, which is both empty and all inclusive.

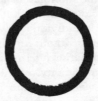

Let us consider the syllable *hūṃ* as in the mantra "*Oṁ mani padme hūṃ*," the middle words of which signify "jewel" (*mani*) and "lotus" (*padme*) — the jewel in the lotus, a union of masculine and feminine principles. This syllable is both a mantra (when pronounced over and over) and a maṇḍala (when its written form is contemplated);

The *h* sound, called the *visarga* (ह), is in the center, surmounted by the *m* sound, really just a vibration of air in a sort of humming fashion, represented by the dot about the visarga, called the *anusvara*. Below is the vowel, without which nothing could be pronounced (ɔ). The visarga and the vowel give us the components of speech, a consonant and a vocalization. Words can be pronounced only when vowels and consonants are united, and in Saiva Siddhanta thought this analogy is used to explain what is called in English Qualified Nondualism. That is, from a theoretical standpoint, vowels and consonants have separate existences, distinguishable from each other, as in a theoretical fashion divinity and humanity can be distinguished, and so can male and female. In actual fact, one cannot function without the other. In English no consonant can be pronounced without a vowel sound. In the Tamil language vowels do not stand alone.

The simple syllable *hūṃ* can be pronounced over and over, but when its symbolism is understood, it can guide the initiate into new birth, for unlike the *h* or the *u*, the *ṁ* is itself a union. From this point of view knowledge (*gnosis*, if you wish) is a "drop," (*bindu*) created by the mingling of the male seed (*sukla*) and the female ovum (*rakta*). That is to say that in the bindu alone is conveyed the knowledge that until one overcomes the polarities of existence, transcending the difference between male and female and all other polarities, gnosis cannot be born.

In Buddhist perfection of wisdom literature (The *Prajñaparamītā*) special attention is paid to nothingness — zero. Early mathematical systems were hampered by the lack of a zero. In Babylonian and Roman numerical systems, only "things" were counted. In the early centuries A.D., the concept of *śuṇya* (nothingness) became an important philosophical consideration in India. European computation systems, based on what are called Arabic numbers, were carried from India to the west by Arabs.

Coomeraswamy is worth quoting on this point. He maintains that to the Indian mind all numbers are virtually or potentially present in that which is without number. ". . . zero is to number as possibility is to actuality."[35] Macy further elaborates, that the use of the term *ananta* ("endless") implies an identification of zero with infinity, in which the beginning of every series is the same as its end. The term *ākāśa* represents a "purely principal space without dimensions."

> This space becomes the still center of the turning world. . . . For the wheel to revolve the center must be empty. From it perhaps the sign for zero came. It is the circle in which end and beginning merge. That zero can also be a sexual sign for the female, suggesting another link between the feminine and the void. . . . Around the *śūnyatā*, which she represents, the Wheel of the Buddha Dharma turns. That void is, as D. T. Suzuki said, "not an abstraction but an experience, or a deed enacted where there is neither space nor time."[36]

Ones and twos are different, in that they separate one existence (lit. "to stand outside") from another. But combining the circle and the dot

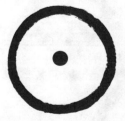

produces an ancient symbol for the cosmos, the ordered world, often associated with the command, "Let there be light."

Already here are the elements of a maṇḍala, but we can go further. A vertical stroke

generally represents godhood, or in some cases masculinity. It pushes heaven and earth apart, and in some schemes is seen as the sacred pole, the axis mundi. The horizontal stroke

is the horizon, already a kind of union and unity, and it represents the *anima*, or the feminine side of life, long associated with wholeness. It is in this area where real creativity lies, probably the reason behind the tantric veneration of female sexuality.

When these two lines are crossed, we have one of the most ancient symbols of wholeness.

It is no accident that the cross became a symbol of wholeness, the expression of new life, with its four dimensions plus a center. It underlies the form of Christian Churches and Hindu temples. The cross was a symbol of unity and restoration of wholeness long before its use in Christianity.

Having seen circles, we can consider triangles. In the East, the upward-pointing triangle was usually seen as symbolic of the masculine,

and the downward triangle of the feminine.

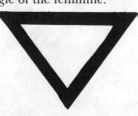

If, however, they are coupled, a new figure is created, more than the sum of the individual parts.

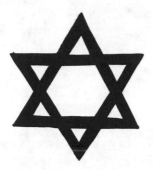

Long before its use in Judaism, this symbol, particularly with a bindu and circle added, stood for the cosmos — my self and the great Self at the center.

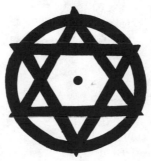

It underlies the Śrī cakra, which appears on page 39. In the words of the Bṛhadāranyaka Upaniṣad,

As all the spokes are connected with the hub and the rim, so all creatures, all gods, all worlds, all organs are bound together in the soul.

A maṇḍala, then, with its five directions, four sides surrounding a center, can be seen as a structure of human personality and of the cosmos. But all this is somewhat external. For the adept no external maṇḍala is needed at all, and one's own spine makes the human body its own maṇḍala.

In some Tantric traditions, especially in what is known as Kundalini Yoga, made popular in America by Gopi Krishna, a huge reserve of spiritual energy is located at the base of the spine. When aroused it can travel upwards through six *cakras*, six maṇḍala centers of varying kinds of energies, finally reaching a seventh at the top of the head. The accompanying diagram shows the several centers, their symbolic shape, and the proper mantric formulae to be used with each. The first cakra, *mūla*, involves the struggle to survive. The second, *svadhiṣṭhāna*, involves sexuality, and the

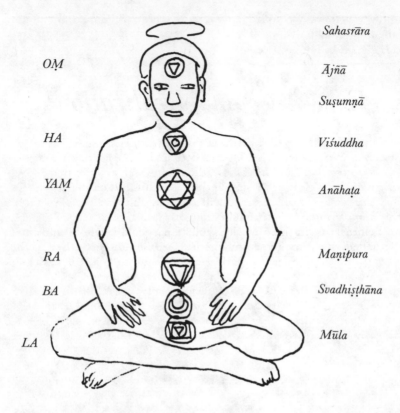

third, *maṇipura*, produces the urge to dominate. These are the three cakras activated by most people.

The next three require spiritual discipline to activate. *Anāhaṭa*, with its union of the two triangles, is the activation of selfless (not romantic) love. *Viśuddha* and *Ājñā*, each with prominent feminine triangles, begin transcendental states of being. If the meditator can reach *sahasrāra*, the bondage of the individual self has vanished. A has united with B, to use a former illustration.

The maṇḍala, when internalized in the meditative process, is a search for solution to what Paul Mus called the "Problematic of the Self." But it must be internalized for this to be the case. A portion of the Tibetan Book of the Dead puts it thus:

> These paradises are not situated elsewhere, they are disposed in the center and at the four cardinal points of thy heart and coming forth from it they appear before thee. These shapes come from no other place; they are solely the fabric of thy mind. As such thou must recognize them. . . .

What an insight into human life!

CHAPTER 6

Experience and Realization

SOME YEARS ago I heard the sainted Swami Akhilananda, head of the Boston and Providence Ramakrishna Vedanta Centers, talk about the "realization of God," and I was mystified: How can anyone make God real? Either he is real or he isn't, and no amount of thinking will affect reality one iota. Common sense tells us that. But that reaction came before any introduction to meditation or spiritual practices. No one taught me — although I had many teachers — but little by little a realization itself overtook my former dogmatism. I came to see for myself that all reality, including God or the gods, is real only when it is realized. This position is not an affront to the truth claim of any religion or the claim of any theology. It is simply to assert that what is "out there" may never be known, and even if it does conform to the accepted dogmas, it is not at this point that it affects human life.

Seen in this way prayer takes on a new dimension. Except for the most myopic literal mind it is hard to conceive of a Being out there who carefully listens to the language addressed to "Him" in prayer, most of it banal and flattering about trivial matters. Long ago I came to the conclusion that God does not speak — or understand — the English language. Neither, then, does he listen to Hebrew, Greek, Sanskrit, or Tamil, and certainly he is not exclusively addicted to Arabic. Then, why pray?

Words used in prayers are important, but their effect is on the person praying. They are necessary mantras to establish a relationship. A relationship between humans withers if words are not used, but woe to any person who trusts the literal denotations of the language of love. The real communication takes place on a level deeper (or higher) than words, and the words are important means to that end, as we have seen in the course of this investigation. Intercessory prayer, then, has a real place, not so much because the contents of the words are weighed by a celestial tribunal but because they put the praying person in touch with cosmic power. Some years ago I received in the same month a card from a dear friend who is a priest in the Roman Catholic Church informing me that on such and such a day, mass would be said in my intention and a letter from another dear friend, a Buddhist bhikkhu informing me that "I visualize you in my meditations." The ontological background and confessional understandings of these two great souls could never be reconciled with each other, but was there such a vast difference in what each of them was doing for me?

Verbal Differences/Spiritual Unities

When you use these films, you can look for certain underlying constant emphases. I find these: authentic immediacy, concentration on the present moment, and relaxed intensity.

The words *authentic* and *immediate* are over-used to the point of becoming banal clichés, but I know nothing to replace them. When the Buddha talked about Right Seeing, I think he meant a sense of authenticity. When Western existentialists talked about it, they had much the same idea. We are constantly bombarded by sense data, and in this sensory overload we lose our way. We substitute labels for reality and formulae for truth. Authentic knowledge is direct, not mediated, hence, *immediate*. The delightful and profound Daisetz T. Suzuki used to love to recite this poem,

> When you see with the ears / and hear with the eyes
>   You cherish no doubts.
> How natural, then, is the rain dropping off the eaves!

I do not know its source. The poem itself makes no sense until one's whole being is concentrated on a single mundane act: raindrops splashing plop, plop, plop on the ground — and there is no other reality. This is the answer to the Zen koan about the meaning of Bodhidharma's (the founder of Zen) coming from the West, answered only by "the cyprus tree in the courtyard."

Consider such an act as the baking of bread. Very little authentic bread, baked with loving care, is available in our stores. Baking requires careful attention to every detail, kneading, setting aside to rise, and other menial tasks like cleaning up. Yeast must work in its own way, and if there is a real relationship between baker and loaf, there will be a delicious result. Suzuki Roshi says,

> Once you know how the dough becomes bread, you will under-
> stand enlightenment. So how this physical body becomes a sage is
> our main interest. We are not so concerned about what flour is, or
> what dough is, or what a sage is. A sage is a sage. Metaphysical ex-
> planations of human nature are not the point.[37]

A New Testament parable continues to intrigue me. The Kingdom of God, Jesus said, is like a woman who takes three measures of yeast and hides them (note the verb) in the loaf until the whole is leavened. The yeast vanishes, but it transforms everything around it. In the same way it takes only a little yeast to change a life and only a few yeasty persons to change society. Too many theologians are like the authors of cookbooks, who never worked in a kitchen.

Concentration on the present moment — to "Be Here Now" to use Ram Das's famous phrase — is another constant theme which we have already discussed at length. Rare is the person who can act with authentic immediacy in the present moment. If this were not so, soporific television, muzak, and other distracting background noises would cease to be commercially successful.

Relaxed intensity — as we have seen, not at all a contradiction in terms — is the other note emphasized in all these films about spiritual practices. It is hard to relax, but only a relaxed person can focus full intensity on the tasks at hand. When poise and equanimity have been lost, intensity also disappears. In one way or another all spiritual practices begin with relaxing exercises, whether in yoga asanas, quiet sitting, or running around a Caitanya shrine, in order that one may concentrate on the present moment in an authentic immediate awareness.

A Western Application

This book has described several films that can be used in connection with a search for understanding of eastern spiritual practices. Do they have any counterpart in the West?

Hinduism and Buddhism in a variety of forms are practiced in the United States in increasing measure, and as Nyanaponika has observed, there is no intrinsic reason why a Gospel from Benares is any more foreign to London (or Manhattan) than a Gospel from Jerusalem. Both are part of the East. Both have been imported and adapted in the western hemisphere. So every major American city has some Hindu and Buddhist centers. Within a few blocks in Washington, D.C. there is the Washington Buddhist Vihāra, a well-established organization, as well as a new Zen meditation center, a Myōhōji of the Nichiren movement, a Vietnamese temple, and a Tibetan Dharmadattu.[38]

But there is a change in the religious climate of the country as a whole. Many thoughtful people — standing firmly on their religious traditions — accept more and more responsibility for their own growth and development. Although loud voices try to turn back to a simpler age when decisions were made for them, and cry out for the Church, or God, or even Nature to make their decisions, an increasing number are realizing with Beatrice Bruteau that,

> Nature is not Someone Else anymore. Nature — in our local region of the universe — has concentrated herself in our human energy, and what Nature does now to advance the evolution will be what we do. We are evolutionary Nature. And even God, we now realize, is not quite such an outsider, at least not to the point of taking our responsibilities for us. Teilhard several times told us, "God makes us make ourselves," but the weight of his word has not yet sunk deep into our minds.

Many of us continue to hope, in more or less hidden ways, that there will still be some special ones who will volunteer to carry the burden of anxiety and insecurity for us, who will do all this frightening thinking and planning and deciding. And we simple people can just go along with whatever they determine. But perhaps the deepest root of our very real fear of the future is that we can no longer look to the outside for authority. Maybe whatever authority there is, is within. Perhaps there is no "outside," as we had previously thought. And if not, there must not be any outsiders. No "others" on whom to put the responsibility, no "They" to follow, no "Them" to blame. It may turn out that we are it in this game of evolving life, and that it is a matter of "all of us together." In Teilhard's words,

"The gates of the future are not thrown open to a few of the privileged nor to one chosen people to the exclusion of all others. They will open to an advance of all together, in a direction in which all together can join and find completion in a spiritual renovation of the earth."

If we modify the popular spiritual in recognition of the interiority of Deity and our own responsibility, we may sing, "We've got all of us together in our hands; we've got the whole world in our hands."[39]

Notes

1. Mary Ann Bowman, *Western Mysticism: A Guide to Basic Works* (Chicago: American Library Association, 1978) is a detailed and adequate bibliography of western contemplative movements. Morton Kelsey, *The Other Side of Silence* (New York: Paulist Press, 1975) is a valuable introduction to Christian spiritual practices. Important comparisons of Christian and Buddhist practices can be found in the writings of the Zen scholar, D. T. Suzuki, *Meditation, Christian and Buddhist* (New York: Harper & Bros., 1957) and in the works of William Johnston, *The Still Point* (New York: Fordham, 1970) and *Christian Zen* (New York: Harper & Row, 1971).

2. The best guide to Buddhist devotional practices in America is Charles S. Prebish, *American Buddhism* (North Scituate MA: Duxbury Press, 1979). Telephone directories of major cities provide local information.

3. Vol. S, p. 621.

4. *Ibid.*, Vol. S, p. 617.

5. Chandogya Upaniṣad (trans., Swami Nikhilananda), VII, i, 1-3. New York: Harper & Row, 1963.

6. See Joachim Wach, *The Comparative Study of Religion* (New York: Columbia University Press, 1951) and Maurice Friedman, *Touchstones of Reality* (New York: Dutton, 1974) and *The Human Way* ("Religion and Human Experience" series, Chambersburg PA: Anima Books, 1981).

7. See Swami Akhilananda, *Hindu Psychology and Its Meaning for the West* (New York: Harper & Bros., 1946) and *Mental Health and Hindu Psychology* (New York: Harper & Row, 1951).

8. A paperbound edition is available as Nanamoli Thera, *Visuddhimagga: The Path of Purification* (Boulder CO: Shambala, 1976). A further discussion of the role of morality will be found in Daniel Goleman, *The Varieties of the Meditative Experience* (New York: E. P. Dutton, 1977), Part I.

9. Joseph Goldstein, *The Experience of Insight* (Santa Cruz: Unity Press, 1976), p. 144.

10. *Ibid.*, p. 4.

11. Shunryu Suzuki, *Zen Mind, Beginner's Mind* (New York & Tokyo: Weatherill, 1979), p. 57f.

12. Daniel Goleman in *Psychology Today*, February 1976, p. 66.

13. Daniel Goleman, *The Varieties of the Meditative Experience* (New York: Dutton, 1977), p. 53.

14. *Ibid.*, p. 55. My debt to Goleman's treatment will be evident throughout this chapter.

15. Swami Vyas Dev, *First Steps to Higher Yoga*, quoted by Daniel Goleman, *Varieties of the Meditative Experience* (New York: Dutton, 1977), p. 76.

16. Quoted from *ibid.*, pp. 78-9. Attention must be called to the classic book by Mircea Eliade, *Yoga: Immortality, and Freedom* (New York: Princeton University Press, Bollingen Series, 1969).

17. From *Man, Myth, and Magic*, p. 1778.

18. For a discussion of the life of the Buddha see Edward J. Thomas, *The Life of the Buddha as Legend and History* (London: Rutledge & Kegan Paul, 1949).

19. Nyanaponika Thera has written eloquently on the *Satipaṭṭhāna Sutta* in *The Heart of Buddhist Meditation* (London: Rider, 1962), and Daniel Goleman (*op. cit.*) makes the *Visuddhimagga* his chief point of departure.

20. Nyanaponika, *op. cit.*, p. 53.

21. Quoted from *ibid.*, p. 67.

22. *Ibid.*, p. 82.

23. L. Austine Waddell, *Tibetan Buddhism* (reprint, New York: Dover, 1972) is a useful source of information.

24. Lee John Woodruffe, *The Garland of Letters* (Madras: Ganesh & Co., 1969), p. 5.

25. Two highly suggestive books on physics from a new perspective can be recommended: Fritjof Capra, *The Tao of Physics* (Boulder: Shambala Press, 1975) and Gary Zukov, *The Dancing Wu Li Masters* (New York: William Morrow, 1979).

26. Walter Spink, "The Cage of Form," in Harry M. Buck and Glen E. Yocum, *Structural Approaches to South India Studies* (Chambersburg PA: *Anima*, 1974).

27. Illustrations from and discussion based on Philip Rawson, *Tantra* (New York: Avon, 1973), Introduction.

28. *Ibid.*, p. 11.

29. Shunga Suzuki, *Zen Mind, Beginner's Mind* (New York & Tokyo: Weatherhill, 1979), p. 29.

30. *Ibid.*, p. 25.

31. Ira Progoff, *The Well and the Cathedral* (New York: Dialogue House, 1977), p. 35.

32. Andrew Reding, "Let Each Jewel Reflect All the Others, Each According to Its Own Faculty . . ." *Anima* 4/2 Spring 1978, p. 18.

33. Giuseppi Tucci, *The Theory and Practice of the Maṇḍala* (London: Rider, 1961). See also Paul Mus, "The Problematic of the Self—West and East, and the Mandala Pattern," Charles A. Moore (Ed.), *Philosophy and Culture: East and West* (Honolulu: University of Hawaii Press, 1962), pp. 594-610.

34. C. G. Jung, *Mandala Symbolism* (Princeton: Princeton University Press, Bollingen Series XX, 1959).

35. A. K. Coomeraswamy, "Kha and Other Words Denoting Zero in Connection with the Metaphysics of Space," *Bulletin of the School of Oriental Studies*, London Institute, Vol. VII, Part 3, 1934, p. 496.

36. Joanna Macy, "Perfection of Wisdom: Mother of all Buddhas," *Anima*, 3/1 Fall, 1976, pp. 77-78.

37. Shunryu Suzuki, p. 56.

38. See Charles S. Prebish, *American Buddhism* (North Scituate MA: Duxbury Press, 1979) for more complete information.

39. "The Whole World: A Convergence Perspective," *Anima* 2/1 Fall, 1977, p. 6.

Audio-Visual Resources

The Use of the Film

The ubiquitous television tube and cinema screen have broken the monopoly of the printed word and the professional lecture as the resource for learning and the expression of scholarship. When sight and sound combine vividly to recreate an experience, students can sense a degree of immediate participation in their subject matter. Colleges and universities have been slow to exploit the potential of what is often referred to in a deprecating way as audio-visual "aids," but outside the classroom the amount of learning that comes through electronic media increases exponentially. We are, therefore, quite well-conditioned to the impact of such direct, nonlinear learning.

For the student of Asian religious traditions films and television tapes offer a welcome added dimension not available in books and journals. Meditation and spiritual practices are, by nature, experiential, and teaching about them presents many of the same difficulties as "teaching" art or music. Imagine trying to become a serious student of Beethoven without ever listening to the Ninth Symphony or studying gothic architecture without even looking at a picture of Chartres. Imagine a course about India with a section on Indian aesthetics, but never a picture of the Taj Mahal or a recording of Ali Akhbar Khan. Yet course after course on the spirituality of India and Japan will be taught from printed material and spoken lectures alone. It's like writing a cookbook without trying the recipes or tasting the food.

Meditation and spiritual practices are elusive. If talking about them doesn't suffice, neither does a proliferation of pictures and sounds. If one could afford the time and the money, a serious student could receive spiritual instruction at an ashram in India or at a Zen monastery in Japan, and after a period of years at least one tradition would be known intimately. Failing that, an extended visit to the great spiritual centers would be useful. But as a tourist we shall see only externalia, and it is very easy to confuse the trappings of devotional practices with the inner experience they express. Films and tapes have this disadvantage also. All that we can see or hear are phenomena, for this is the meaning of the word *phenomenon*, externalia. It is easy to photograph a Buddhist festival or a Hindu pūja, but the exotic rituals seen and heard — and if one is present, smelled and touched, perhaps tasted — can become so interesting in their own right that we fail to remember that this is only the external expression of a human experience. If we can work our way through the phenomena to the experience as best we can reconstruct it, we may find it not so exotic after all. The idiom of expression must not stand in the way of our appreciating the experience itself.

Right here is the most insidious danger in the use of films in studying religious cultures other than our own. Cultural idioms are fascinating, and what's more, they are photogenic and recordable. It is easy to be side-tracked from a serious concern with meditation and spiritual practices. Films provide access to experiential data in a unique fashion, and independent learners can take full advantage, but without adequate preparation — that is, without a solid background of reading about Buddhism or Hinduism and without reading some of the texts themselves — distortion is inevitable. This guide is prepared to make films accessible and avoid these pitfalls.

There is another difficulty as well. Television and cinema are associated in our minds with the category *The New York Times* calls "Arts and Leisure." By association, television comes to mean relaxation, and the movies equals a night out; serious work is left behind in both cases. We are writing in this book not about arts and leisure but about the art of concentrated looking and listening. Viewing these films is not to be thought of as going to a show. We want to learn to "read" these films with as much sophistication as we need to understand serious books. Sophisticated viewing, like sophisticated reading, is not the same as watching a television show or skimming the Reader's Digest condensation of a book.*

Because we have not been trained in these techniques, motion pictures are classified in most academic institutions as mere audio-visual "aids," and taken as a kind of amusement device to entertain students and release teachers from serious preparation. The more verbally oriented the discipline, the more likely pictures will be thought frivolous or threatening. In the field of religion studies, professors of Judaism, Christianity, and Islam — all called "religions of the Book" — resist the introduction of such materials, and as a rule of thumb, the more prestigious the institution, the less provision it will have for adequately viewing a film or listening to a quality reproduction of a tape. This guide, however, suggests that an afternoon in the viewing room can be as intellectually demanding as a day in the library stacks. It provides suggestions as to the most suitable material and instructions on its effective use.

To students and their teachers alike there are some admonitions. In the previous essay on meditation and spiritual practices references were made to various films, all of which are described in greater detail in this section of the guide. A careful perusal of this section will help you know which ones you want to see and where they can be obtained. Some of these films are entertaining. Many provide a pleasant viewing experience. A few are

*See Melvin E. Levison, "Visual Literacy is Not Enough," *Focus*, IV/2. Winter, 1978, for a full description of these principles.

even very well produced. But your aesthetic enjoyment, although important, is serendipity. Even the film that is not well-done and whose narration you may firmly reject can have value. You must look with a very critical eye.

Because films used in this fashion are a kind of surrogate for personal experience, there is an added risk. The eyes of the camera and the ears of the microphone are not our eyes and ears. We are at the mercy of a film director, a producer, a camera operator, and a film editor, and their points of view have determined what we shall see and hear. We are not free to go down the side street of which we caught a fleeting glimpse as the camera panned around the corner. Even so, if we look carefully, we can see beyond the biases of our filmmakers. To do it, however, requires preparation.

Viewing these films is a kind of meditative experience itself, for it requires careful concentration. Ask the question, what do we see? What do we really see? What else is there to be seen? What did we hear? What did we really hear? What else is there to hear if we listen more carefully? From there we go on to interpretation. Most films are over-narrated. You might want to run through sections of the film with the narration turned off and then see whether you agree with what the narrator has said. There may be room for quite a bit of variance in interpretation of the phenomena, and the more you have read the better you will be able to interpret.

Do not be afraid of your own experiences and sensations. Are you revolted by what you see? Does it look idiotic? Are you so attracted to some charismatic leader that you would, if you could, sell your goods and seek the person out? Why? Learn to ask what it is out there that makes you feel the way you do, and, if you are up to the threat, go on to ask what in your own background and experience produces such an emotional response. Clearly we are discussing more than one casual viewing.

The teacher has an additional responsibility. Films are never a substitute for adequate preparation; indeed, they may demand more of your energy than the preparation of a lecture. You need to be thoroughly familiar with the film you show. You must know when to use the narration on the sound track and when to interject your own interpretation.

For fuller information about any of the films mentioned here, consult the larger works in this series, *Focus on Hinduism* and *Focus on Buddhism*.

The Art of Meditation
    28 minutes, 16mm/color   Sale $300.00
                                                    Rental $35.00
    Films for a New Age, Hartley Productions, Inc., Cat Rock Road,
    Cos Cob, CT 06807

As Allen Watts said, "Reality can't be described — only by silencing the mind, through meditation, can one grasp what reality really is." This film was designed to enable the viewer to rid the mind of all the words and calculations that are going on inside one's head and silence the mind in order to meditate. Emphasis is placed on the importance of breathing as part of the process. Through this process one can arrive at the meditative state where there is no difference between the person and the universe. A oneness exists, and the individual can enter into "what is" at the moment.

This film deals solely with the meditative experience and seems to be closely related to Gestalt Psychology that emphasizes the "now" of all experiences. Such visual images as flowing water and the waves washing over protruding rocks in the sea tend to reinforce what is being said about the meditative experience. The film has a way of capturing the experience itself.

There is a sudden reversal at the end because Watts includes laughter as part of the meditative experience. The laughter seems to bring the film to its conclusion on a positive note. The sound of the laughter may remind us that life is not meant to be taken too seriously. It would seem that anyone who can become so caught up in such a joyous experience is participating in the "now" and is fully involved in life itself.

This film can be used as an introduction to the whole subject of meditation. It will be most effective if it is shown, then discussed, then shown again, because some students will react negatively at first and others whose reactions were positive will become critical on the second showing. Such an interpretation will be needed because of the presentation's one decisive weakness: The style of meditation discussed is the eclecticism of Alan Watts, and it is not tied to any specific school of meditative insight.

Aura of Divinity
    Part I. The nature of the avatar as foretold by ancient prophecies
        36 min. super-8/color with sound $165.00
            two 400-foot reels
        36 min. 16mm/color   1600 feet $275.00
    Part II. The nature of the avatar as explained in the words of Bhagavan
        Sri Sathya Sai Baba.
        36 min. super-8/color $165.00
            two 400-foot reels
        36 min. 16mm/color   1600 feet $275.00
    Spiritual Advancement of the Individual (SAI) Foundation,
    7911 Willoughby Avenue, Los Angeles CA 90046

This is one of the few films available both in a 16mm format and in super-8 sound format. Reel I of the super-8 version opens with shots of outer space, reminding one of a science fiction movie. The narration develops the concepts of messiah, prophet, and avatar, focusing on the life of Sathya Sai Baba, born November 23, 1926 in Tirupathi in South India. His story is told as from his own lips, and many claims are made on his behalf, including the presentation of Sai Baba as the chosen avatar for this degenerate age of *Kali Yuga.* Except as background to the person of the bhagavan, Reel I has little relevance for the study of meditation.

Reel II, however, is considerably more useful. Although continuing to develop claims for the divinity of Sai Baba, there are interesting presentations of mantras, with a good narration on the nature of sound and vibrations, with references to certain modern scientific theories. A pūja room is shown, and there is a discussion on the use of idols, amulets, talismans, and other externalia of religious devotion. An important discussion on the control of bodily functions and an attempted psychological explanation for miraculous and supernatural occurrences is useful, even though it will be controversial for most western viewers.

Although Part II contains some good photographs of meditation, it is not useful in this context.

Awakening
   30 min.   16 mm   videotape version also available
   Lewis Buchner, 253 Capp Street, San Francisco CA 94110

This film details the work of Sri Chinmoy (b. 1931). It can introduce students to an American-based form of Hindu spiritual practices. In most courses the film will have limited usage, but it can serve as the basis for a discussion of the impact of Eastern meditative techniques in the West.

Buddhism: Be Ye Lamps Unto Yourselves
   29 min.   16mm/color   1973   Sale $415.00
                                          Rental $28.00
   Producer: Howard Enders for ABC Series: Directions
   Distributor: Knox Films and University Film Center, University of
      Illinois, Champaign IL 61820

A generalized treatment of basic Buddhism on an elementary level, more suited for a general television audience than a classroom. Although it stresses the Buddhist ideal that no one can purify another, it cannot be used to teach spiritual practices.

Buddhism: Footprint of the Buddha — India
   54 min   16mm/color   1977   Sale $800.00
                                          Rental $100.00
   ¾" Video Cassette, Sale $200.00
   ½" Video Cassette, Sale $150.00
   Time-Life Video, P. O. Box 644, Paramus, New Jersey 07652

"The Long Search" series, narrated by Ronald Eyre, produced for the BBC and widely viewed on television, is an unusually successful presentation of the human experience of religion. This film is one of the thirteen presentations in the series. The professional quality of production is apparent at every step, and it can be used effectively in the classroom and by independent viewers, as it allows viewers an opportunity to capture the feeling of Buddhism as lived among the monks and laity of Sri Lanka. One can catch a glimpse of the life of the monks who live in cities and towns, monks who live in forests, a young boy about to become a novice, and some of the laity. Also, one can capture something of the significance of the rain retreat, a celebration that monks prepare for in order to welcome the laity when they arrive.

In addition to providing information about the Buddha and about Theravāda Buddhism, Buddhist spiritual practices are developed in some detail. Chanting the Three Refuges in a Buddhist "Sunday School" shows the doctrine of impermanence and points the way to nirvāṇa. Temples are shown as places of worship without an altar, without a dividing line with God on one side and the devotees on the other, and there is a valuable sequence on how to look at a statue.

Meditation is sensitively shown. The first lesson comes when a young boy prepares for the monkhood, having his hair shaved. The emptiness of the meditation room is used as an illustration of the emptiness needed in the consciousness of the meditator. Forest monks show the importance of controlled mindfulness, "When you are walking, know that you are walking, and when you are breathing, know that you are breathing."

More than one viewing is desirable.

Buddhism: Land of the Disappearing Buddha — Japan
    54 min.   16mm/color   **Sale $750.00**
                                                   Rental $100.00
    ¾ " Video Cassette, Sale $200.00
    ½ " Video Cassette, Sale $150.00
    Time-Life Video, P. O. Box 644, Paramus, New Jersey 07652

As part of the very successful "Long Search" series, this production shows professional competence throughout in its sophisticated narration, photography, and editing. Ronald Eyre, the narrator, stresses the point that Buddhism in Japan does not appear as a separate element of life, but the Buddha has disappeared into a total Japanese experience; hence, the otherwise irrelevant shots of Tokyo's crowded traffic.

There are some choice moments: a fencing scene ("Put the whole of yourself into one undeflected blow"), calligraphy, archery, a striking photograph of a rainbow at Mount Fuji, Pure Land chanting ("not prayers to a god for what he will do but thanks to the Buddha for what he has done.") and a tea ceremony. Although these episodes are tantalizingly brief, individually and collectively they would be useful in discussing meditation and spiritual practices. The narrative stresses the present moment ("Be all there, not passing through on the way to somewhere else.") and the realization of one's own nature as the Buddha nature. Meditation is practiced in a factory and in a restaurant. Some will object to the overly-dramatic use of the *kyosaku* (the stick used to aid Zen meditation), but on the whole the presentations are well-balanced.

Zen traditions form an underlying motif, but Pure Land practices are given careful treatment, and there is an instructive section on the Nichiren Shoshu Sokagakkai.

Buddhism: The Path to Enlightenment
30 min.   16mm/color   Sale $350.00
                                                 Rental $35.00
Films for a New Age, Hartley Productions, Inc., Cat Rock Road,
Cos Cob, CT 06807

Although externalia are displayed constantly, this beautifully photographed film shows some lay practices of Buddhism: offerings of flowers and lights, veneration of images, meditation in monasteries, and processions. Unfortunately, the narration is superficial and condescending, but much of the film may be used profitably without the sound track.

A Contemporary Guru: Rajnish
Videotape available from
University of Wisconsin — Madison, Department of South Asian Studies
1242 Van Hise Hall, 1220 Linden Drive, Madison WI 53706

An interesting study of the effect of a contemporary charismatic spiritual leader in a presentation that illustrates the role of the teacher in effectively transmitting a tradition and the place of ecstasy or altered states of consciousness. There are some healing exorcisms and a short section on sufi practices. Considerable attention is given to relaxation and control of bodily and mental energy. This is one film that could, in fact, substitute for a lecture.

The Flow of Zen
14 min.   16mm/color   Sale $200.00
                                                 Rental $25.00
Films for a New Age, Hartley Productions, Inc., Cat Rock Road,
Cos Cob CT 06807

This film has been described as a "mood film in which Alan Watts interprets life's experience in Taoist terms." Most of the photography is abstract, colored water flowing and swirling, providing a sensuous experience which may contribute to a feeling about the ever-changing realities of experience, God, and nature. Beyond the creation of a mood, there is little here of use in understanding meditation and spiritual practices.

Hinduism and the Song of God
30 min.   16mm/color   Sale $325.00
                                                 Rental $35.00
Films for a New Age, Hartley Productions, Inc., Cat Rock Road,
Cos Cob CT 06807

A popular film in many college courses, *Hinduism and the Song of God* deserves attention in any course dealing with Asian religious practices. The title is taken from the *Bhagavad Gītā*, but there is little further reference to Kṛṣṇa's great song. The film's central section deals with the three yogas (margas): *karma*, the way of works; *jñāna*, the way of contemplation and study; and *bhakti*, the way of devotion. In trying to present the whole range of Hinduism in half an hour this presentation falls into the same trap experienced by the casual visitor to India: the beautiful life of affluent urban Indians becomes the norm.

If a class is properly prepared, however, certain short vignettes can be useful. There are brief but dramatic presentations of ritual bathing, cholam-drawing (the intricate designs appearing on floors) hatha yoga postures, life in an ashram, pilgrimage, pūja, and even a yogin sitting on a bed of nails. Students could then recognize and identify many of the external aspects of Hindu spiritual practices previously discussed.

Hinduism: Many Paths to God
    Xerox Films, 1250 Fairwood Avenue, Columbus OH 43216

This film illustrates the journey of a holy man. Set in a remote mountain gorge, the yogin begins his day at the Ganges, the holiest of rivers. For forty years the yogin has meditated on a rock along the Ganges. He follows the path of knowledge in order to escape the cycle of rebirth while most people follow the path of faith.

The viewer is acquainted with some of the many facets of Hinduism. The religion is described as polytheistic; however, there is a strong element of monotheism within it. Each person chooses his/her own deity from the many gods and goddesses. Many people worship Durga, the mother goddess, while Kṛṣṇa is considered the most human and loveable of the gods. The narrator describes four stages of man's spiritual life as that of a student, householder, moving away from earthly possessions and, lastly, that of an ascetic.

An interview with a Hindu scholar reveals what is behind the popularity of the religion among Western nations. Hinduism is an open religion and stresses the individual's relationship to duty. Westerners come in search of a part of Hinduism in order to solve their psychological problems. They seek a guru who is seldom the source of their faith.

This film effectively presents the worship and meditated experiences of the holy man as a representative of Hinduism.

I Am a Monk
    30 min.   16mm/color   **Sale $325.00**
                                                          Rental $35.00
    Films for a New Age, Hartley Productions, Inc., Cat Rock Road,
       Cos Cob, CT 06807

A charming story of a young American, Michael (Mike), who is disillusioned with western culture and finds refuge in a Thai Buddhist monastery. In his own words, Mike describes the inner meaning of meditation as awareness that begins from within and goes outward. There are the usual shots of feet in walking meditation and a brief glimpse of chanting. In the film, Mike visits his parents in America and tries to explain to them his new way of life as a beggar (*bhikkhu*). We are treated to some of his problems, e.g., the difficulty of writing to his former girlfriends and signing the letters "Love, Mike."

The story reflects the rebellious mood of the 60s and implicitly recommends rejection of Western culture to seek refuge in Theravāda Buddhism. If this film is used in class, some exposure to the practices of Buddhist monks should precede it, and students should read some Theravāda literature, perhaps the *Satipaṭṭhāna Sutta* itself or at least some of the excellent pamphlets distributed by the Buddhist Publication Society.

Meditation Crystallized
13 min.   16mm/color   1973   Sale $200.00
**   Rental $25.00**
Hartley Film Foundation, Cat Rock Road, Cos Cob CT 06807

Neither this film nor *Requiem for a Faith* will be entirely satisfactory in describing Tibetan meditative and spiritual practices, but better material seems to be nonexistent. *Meditation Crystallized* can serve as an introduction to Tibetan Buddhist art and its function in the spiritual life. The narrator, Lama Govinda, has an important discussion on the way in which supernatural beings, demons, or angels, are crystallizations of the consciousness of the meditator. He also has some important comments on the use of maṇḍalas. Because the film requires only thirteen minutes, it can be the basis for a lively class discussion.

The Path
33 min.   16mm/color   Sale $345.00
**   Rental $35.00**
**   ($15.50 from Univ. of Ill.)**
Sumai Films
University Film Center, University of Illinois, Champaign IL 61820

The tea ceremony provides a beautiful illustration of Japanese spiritual practices. It requires no temple, no priesthood, no cult — except the cult of tea itself. Here is an exquisite presentation, ideally suited to sophisticated classroom use — but not, definitely not, without adequate preparation.

Whereas most documentaries are overnarrated, this one has long periods of silence, relieved only by the sound of pouring water or the swish of mixing the tea. The scene is an actual tea ceremony, with the camera placed at about the level of the viewer's eyes, were he or she present in the ceremony. Because words are at a minimum, and the way of tea itself is the teacher, the film demonstrates its own thesis: only by careful observation does one learn. Viewing this motion picture, then, comes close to actual participation in a well-conducted Japanese tea ceremony. For this reason, unless the viewer is prepared to enter into the experience as an experience and not to watch a film for entertainment, *The Path* will be interminably boring. With adequate preparation and anticipation, however, participation in the film can be a spiritual experience.

A detailed guide has been prepared to accompany the film, "Japanese Tea: The Ritual, The Aesthetics, The Way," available from MSS Information Corporation, 655 Madison Avenue, New York NY 10021.

Requiem for a Faith
28 min.   16mm/color   Sale $300.00
                                                  Rental $35.00
Hartley Film Foundation, Cat Rock Road, Cos Cob CT 06807

The volume *Focus on Buddhism* discusses twenty films on Himālayan religious practices, but none of them are adequate for serious classroom use in describing Tibetan meditation. This film does show some Tibetan Buddhist practices as practiced a decade ago by refugees in North India. A large portion of the footage is taken up with rotating designs that have little meaning, during Huston Smith's narration. If used in connection with *Meditation Crystallized*, the combined effect can be useful.

The Smile
20 min.   16mm/color   Out of print
University of Wisconsin — Madison, Department of South Asian
    Studies, 1242 Van Hise Hall, 1220 Linden Drive, Madison WI 53706

Although this charming film will hold the viewer's interest, it is of limited use for the study or experience of spiritual practices. It depicts Burmese Buddhism through the eyes of a young novice accompanying the Venerable Narada, and its strengths lie in the little details: touching a buffalo, observing a worm, and so on.

Zen in Life
25 min.   16mm/color   1967   Rental $27.00
University of California — Berkeley

Soto Zen discipline and practice is the subject of this film made at the temple monasteries of Eiheiji and So-ji-ji. Meditative practices and the carefully regulated lives of Zen monks is clearly and sensitively shown.

Zen in Ryoku-in
71 min.   16mm/color   Sale $595.00
                                                  Rental $55.00
Ruth Stephan Films

This rather long film is a sensitive portrayal of the daily routine in a small Zen temple in Kyoto, Japan. The narrator, Ruth Stephan, a poet, stresses the relation of Zen to the arts and aesthetics of Japan in general. Although this film will hold the viewer's interest because of its beautiful portrayal of artistic motifs, it does little for the serious student of spiritual practices. Unless this film is used for other purposes also, *Zen in Life* may be a better choice.

Vejen
    22 min.   16mm/color   Sale $275.00
                                                            Rental $10.55
    Carousel Films, 1501 Broadway, New York NY 10036

This film, like *The Smile*, depicts Burmese Buddhism through the eyes of a young boy, attendant to a monk. It is sensitively done, but of limited use for the topic of this study.

Bibliography

This bibliography is not intended to be inclusive. It is simply a listing of those books that will be helpful in developing the topics discussed in this volume.

Akhilananda, Swami. *Hindu Psychology and Its Meaning for the West*. New York: Harper & Bros., 1946.

_____. *Mental Health and Hindu Psychology*. New York: Harper & Row, 1951.

Arberry, A. J. *Sufism, An Account of the Mystics of Islam*. London: Allen & Unwin, 1970.

Argüelles, José and Miriam. *Mandala*. Berkeley and London: Shambala, 1972.

Blofeld, John. *Mantras: Sacred Words of Power*. New York: E. P. Dutton, 1977.

_____. *The Zen Teaching of Hui Hai*. London: Rider, 1962.

Bowman, Mary Ann. *Western Mysticism: A Guide to Basic Works*. Chicago: American Library Association, 1978.

Capra, Fritjof. *The Tao of Physics*. Boulder: Shambala Press, 1975.

Chogyam Trungpa. *Cutting Through Spiritual Materialism*. Boulder: Shambala Press, 1973.

_____. *Meditation in Action*. Boulder: Shambala Press, 1970.

_____. *The Myth of Freedom and the Way of Mindfulness*. Boulder: Shambala Press, 1976.

Dogen. *A Primer of Soto Zen*. Honolulu: University of Hawaii Press, 1971.

Eliade, Mircea. *Yoga, Immortality, and Freedom*. Princeton: Princeton University Press, Bollingen Series, 1958.

Ellwood, Robert S., Jr. *Mysticism and Religion*. Englewood Cliffs: Prentice-Hall, 1980.

Evans-Wentz, W. Y. *The Tibetan Book of the Dead*. London: Oxford University Press.

_____. *The Tibetan Book of the Great Liberation*. London: Oxford University Press, 1969.

_____. *Tibetan Yoga and Secret Doctrines*. London: Oxford University Press, 1958.

Friedman, Maurice. *Touchstones of Reality*. New York: Dutton, 1974.

Goldstein, Joseph. *The Experience of Insight*. Santa Cruz: Unity Press, 1976.

Goleman, Daniel. *Varieties of the Meditation Experience*. New York: Dutton, 1977.

Iyengar, B. K. S., *Light on Prānāyāma: The Yogic Art of Breathing*. New York: Crossroads Press, 1981.

Johnston, William. *The Still Point*. New York: Fordham University Press, 1970.

Jung, C. G. *Mandala Symbolism*. Princeton: Princeton University Press, Bollingen Series XX, 1959.

Kasulis, T. P. *Zen Action Zen Person*. Honolulu: University of Hawaii Press, 1981.

Kelsey, Morton. *The Other Side of Silence*. New York: Paulist Press, 1975.

Kornfield, Jack. *Living Buddhist Masters*. Santa Cruz: Unity Press, 1977.

Nyanaponika Thera. *The Heart of Buddhist Meditation*. London: Rider, 1962.

Prebish, Charles S. *American Buddhism*. North Scituate MA: Duxbury Press, 1979.

Progoff, Ira. *The Well and the Cathedral*. New York: Dialogue House, 1977.

Rahula, Walpole. *What the Buddha Taught*. New York: Grove, 1974.

Rawson, Philip. *Tantra: The Indian Cult of Ecstasy*. New York: Avon, 1973.

Suzuki, Daisetz T. *Meditation, Christian and Buddhist*. New York: Harper & Bros., 1957.

_____. *Essays in Zen Buddhism (Second Series)*. London: Rider, 1949.

Suzuki, Shunryu. *Zen Mind, Beginner's Mind*. New York & Tokyo: Weatherill, 1979.

Tucci, Giuseppi. *The Theory and Practice of the Maṇḍala*. London: Rider, 1961.

Visuddhimagga (tr. Nanamoli Thera). Boulder: Shambala Press, 1976.

The Buddhist Publication Society in Kandy, Sri Lanka, publishes an excellent series of small pamphlets. For information consult the Buddhist Vihara Society, Inc., 5017 16th Street NW, Washington DC 20011. Special attention is called to the following titles:

Khantipālo, Bhikkhu. *Practical Advice for Meditators*.

Goleman, Daniel. *The Buddha on Meditation and Higher States of Consciousness*.

Piyadassi Thera. *The Seven Factors of Enlightenment*.

Nyanasatta Thera. *The Foundations of Mindfulness* (Satipaṭṭhāna Sūtta).

Swearer, Donald K. *A Guide to the Perplexed*.

Glossary

It is impossible to discuss Hindu and Buddhist spiritual practices without technical terms that frequently suffer from English translation. This glossary identifies certain key terms with a brief explanation or definition, rarely with a direct English equivalent. Terms are drawn chiefly from Sanskrit, Pāli, and Japanese languages. Because the Roman alphabet used for the English language is insufficient to accommodate all the characters used in writing these languages, certain diacritical marks are used. There is wide variation in the way in which many of these terms are transliterated into English. Spellings here conform to widely used scholarly practice.

Amida	One of the forms of Buddhahood in Japanese Mahāyāṇa, a dhyana Buddha, who will conduct the faithful to a Pure Land. Amida, known as O-mi-to in Chinese, is the center of devotion of Pure Land cults venerated by the mantra, "Namu Amida Butsu."
anātta	(Pāli spelling for Sanskrit *anātman*). The doctrine that there is no individual personality (*ātman*). Central to most Buddhist doctrine, but stressed particularly in the Theravāda.
anicca	A parallel Buddhist doctrine that nothing is permanent.
arahant	An enlightened being in Theravāda Buddhism. The goal of much Theravāda meditation is arahantship.
āsana	Varous postures in Patanjali's Yoga system.
bhakti	Loving devotion to a particular deity. One of the three standard Hindu yogas.
bhikkhu/bhikkuni	Ascetic Theravāda Buddhists, roughly equivalent terms to "monk" and "nun."
bodhisattva	In Theravāda Buddhism, the Buddha before he became Buddha. In the Mahāyāṇa, a being who has withheld his own salvation until all the world can be redeemed.
cakra	Circle or wheel. In Tantra there are seven cakras located along the human spine.
dukkha	The first of the Four Truths of Buddhism: life is unsatisfactory, and we are in fact suffering.
guru	A spiritual teacher.
hatha	The physical side of Hindu yoga.
Hinayāna	The lesser vehicle. A somewhat pejorative term frequently used for Theravāda Buddhism in contrast to Mahāyāṇa.
jhana	Altered states of consciousness. Stages on the way to one-pointedness.

jñāna	Knowledge gained by contemplation and study. One of the three standard Hindu yogas.
Jodo and Jodo-Shin	Two of the most important Pure Land Buddhist denominations in Japan.
Kabbalah	The mystic form of Judaism. Also its literature.
karma	Deeds and actions. The doctrine of karma stresses that every action, including thought, has an effect, and every effect a cause. *Karmayoga* is also one of the three standard Hindu yogas.
kyosaku	The stick used in Zen meditations to help a monk concentrate.
koan	An unanswerable riddle used in Zen spirituality.
Mahāyāṇa	The "Great Vehicle" school of Buddhism stressing the ideal of the bodhisattva as opposed to the ideal of the arahant.
mantra	A verbal formula to be repeated either to release power or to focus concentration.
marga	A way or a path. In Hinduism there are three standard margas (also called *yogas*): *bhakti, karma, and jñāna.* Some yogis and yoga texts include a fourth: *raja yoga.*
prāṇa	Breath.
pūja	A general term in Hinduism and Buddhism for ritual worship either in a temple or at home.
raja	Royal yoga. *Raja* is Sanskrit for "king."
samādhi	Used in Yoga to mean absorption, the goal of the process. Elsewhere it is the ultimate spiritual realization, release from *saṃsāra.*
saṃsāra	The interdependent process of death, rebirth, life, old age and death. All beings are caught in *saṃsāra* until they find release.
Satipaṭṭhāna Sūtta	A basic meditation text in the Theravāda tradition.
Shingon	One of the schools of esoteric, or True Word Buddhism in Japan.
siṣya	The student of a guru.
Śrī cakra	A complex diagram of interlaced triangles used in goddess worship in Hinduism.
Sufi	A Muslim mystic.
Tendai	One of the schools of esoteric, or True Word Buddhism, in Japan.
Theravāda	That form of Buddhism that stresses arahantship and self-purification. Found chiefly in South and Southeast Asia.
Tipitaka	(Pali for Sanskrit *Tripitaka*). The threefold canonical scripture of the Theravāda.
Vipassana	"Insight" meditation in Theravāda Buddhism.
Visuddhimagga	A basic meditation text in the Theravāda tradition.
Yoga	A spiritual discipline. The equivalent of *marga.* The system of spiritual practices taught by Patanjali.
Zazen	The method of Zen meditation in Japan.